WOOD, LUCK & SURVIVAL

*The Journey of a Father and his Son
through the holocaust Horrors*

REUVEN (GUTKIN) GOVRIN

This book is dedicated to the memory of the Gutkin, Schalman and Rogalin family members that lost their lives and did not survive the Holocaust.

Wood, Luck & Survival
Reuven (Gutkin) Govrin

Translation from the Hebrew: Danny Bar On

ISBN 978-1985356726

WOOD, LUCK & SURVIVAL

The Journey of a Father and his Son through the Holocaust Horrors

REUVEN (GUTKIN) GOVRIN

Contents

Memory is the diary that we all carry about with us.

- Oscar Wilde

INTRODUCTION

I CANNOT REMEMBER A THING

Sunday, October 5, 1997
At the crossroads of Brīvības 88 and Matisa streets, Riga, Latvia

Brivibas Street (Brīvības Iela) is the main street crossing Riga, the capital of Latvia. The street snakes through the entire town and climbs very gradually to the North-East, from the old town beside the Daugava River to the outskirts. On either side of the street that crosses the town center stand five or six-story luxurious houses in yellow, gray, brown and black, situated just above an endless avenue of stores.

After just a fifteen-minute stroll along the street, passing the Old City and the green parks that surround it, Brivibas Street intersects with Matisa Street (Matisa Iela), Miera Street (Miera Iela) and Charlotte Street (Šarlotes Iela), an intersection which creates an open space that breaks the monotony of the buildings along the street.

Close by, on the north side of the street, a black and bronze statue can be seen - a figure with a wrinkled, ascetic face and hooded, sunken eyes. The figure is bald, but has a beard and a sprout of long hair hanging from the back of his neck.

The statue sits cross-legged and upright, and the artist has sculpted a whiteboard and a paintbrush on its chiseled thighs. This is a statue of the painter Irbe. Passersby have laid bouquets of fresh red, yellow and pink flowers on Irbe's sculpted legs.

Right in front of Irbe's statue stands the house on 88 Brivibas Street - a large corner building with four wings, which together create a rectangular shape like the Hebrew letter Final Mem (ם), with a large courtyard in the center. One wing faces Brivibas Street, another faces Matisa Street, and there are two additional internal wings. There are shops at street level, with over five residential floors above. Over the top residential floor facing Brivibas Street stands a cone-shaped spire, topped by a gray metal dome. The entire house is painted in a faded light gray.

In one corner of the building, there is a passage to the internal courtyard which is five meters wide, with a six-meter-high arch-shaped ceiling. On the opposite corner of the building there is another passage, almost identical to the other. As I was standing in one of these passages, stretching an imaginary line diagonally across the inner courtyard, it was suddenly split into two equal triangles.

The building rises above all the surrounding areas, and anyone that passes by cannot help but be greatly impressed by it. It takes only a casual glance at the building to realize that the original occupants were wealthy, high-class individuals. Impressive stone carvings adorn the outer walls of the building, and two sculpted heads of roaring lions guard the two passages and entrances to the courtyard. A figure of a little girl with pigtails is sculpted above each of the roaring lions' heads.

'Before the War', my father grew up in apartment no. 11, the large apartment on the first residential floor of this building. Many years have passed, many things have happened, and many people have died since then. Inside the apartment, almost nothing remains as it was before the war. So, Except for red wallpaper with burgundy moldings, which my father's mother had pasted in 1938 especially for his Bar Mitzvah party. The wallpaper is still on the living room walls.

Other people have lived in apartment no. 11 since then, so during our visit to Riga in October 1997, my father and I did not stay there. We chose to stay in a small one-room apartment behind the pharmacy at the far end of the courtyard. It was as if we were hiding from the present; hiding from the memory of the past buried in the silent walls of the building.

It was a Sunday when my father and I went out early in the morning to visit the city of Riga. We crossed the inner courtyard and went to the main street through the Northwest Passage. The street was empty of cars. We saw two elderly people walking slowly in the distance. Except for them, there was no one else on the street. The people of Riga used the opportunity to sleep in on the weekend. The sky was blue, and the cozy sun warmed the cool autumn air of the early morning. There was a very relaxing feeling in the air. Even the flowers that had been placed at the foot of Irbe's statue that week looked more colorful than ever.

My father crossed the street, stood in front of Irbe's statue and said, "Robby, I actually knew him. He looked just like the sculpture. When I was a child, we thought he was crazy and we used to run after him. Sometimes my father, your grandfather, Samuel, would give me a coin so I could give it to Irbe. Irbe would smile at me and shake his head. He was a really weird person, but we children loved to stand and watch him. I remember..." continued my father, a small smile on his face and his eyes staring into the distance, "... he used to walk barefoot all year long, even in winter, even when it was really cold, and the street was covered with snow. He was very weird..."

I was not surprised when I heard that detailed description; poor memory was never a problem for my father. I looked at the statue of the old painter's figure again and noticed for the first time that the artist had chosen to memorialize him barefoot.

We began walking down the street towards the Daugava River. After a few minutes, my father stopped near a tall, sinister looking building and muttered quietly, "The headquarters of the KGB was right here in this brown, eerie building, just after the Russian invasion of Latvia. Later, it was the Gestapo headquarters and when the Russians returned, it was used again as the KGB's headquarters." It really is a scary building, I thought to myself. We continued a little longer and then we stopped again. My father pointed to one of the buildings and said, "My friend Fima Feldhuhn lived in this house, and in the house right across the corner lived the Shomer family, whose daughter Ruth was in my class at the Jewish school." We continued on our way, enjoying the warm sun, until we reached a beautiful green park, the Esplanāde, down the street. We sat down on a park bench for a rest.

While enjoying the splendor of the winter sun, I felt it

might be the right moment. I turned to my father and said, "Daddy, you've told me so much about what happened before the War and a lot about what happened after the War, but I know nothing about what happened to you during the War. You are no longer a young man, and who knows if you will have the opportunity to ever tell us about it. We're in Riga now, where it all happened. Please tell me what happened to you during the War. How did you survive?" I felt stressed, almost breathless, awaiting his response.

My Father did not respond immediately. After what felt like an eternity, he turned towards me, looked at me with that penetrating look of his through his thick-lensed spectacles, and told me in a low, quiet voice, "Robby, when the War was over and we found out there was almost nothing left, I had to make a decision; to go and avenge those who murdered my family and probably be killed myself, or to forget, and go on living. So I decided to forget. I cannot remember a thing! And that's it." He turned his face toward the park and after a few moments, he motioned me with his hand that it was time to continue our walk. We got up, and nothing else was said on this subject.

This, of course, was not the first time that my father had been asked to tell the story of how he and his father survived the Holocaust; the only ones from the large Gutkin family who lived in Latvia before World War II. My younger brother Assa and I had been trying for many years to make him talk, but without success. We never lost our curiosity, but there was nothing we could do about it. His biography during the years 1941-1945, the years of the War, was a distant and unknown world with a forbidden entrance.

Two years earlier, in 1995, my father had celebrated his seventieth birthday. On the occasion of that event, Assa suggested to my father that he should record his experiences during the years of the War directly into a recording device, without the presence of any of us. Assa thought that perhaps my father would find it easier to tell his story this way. My father had asked for a short time to think about the suggestion and after a few days he declined, offering no explanation - simply "No"!

Over the years we have gathered bits of information, but we've never figured out how to piece them together, nor managed to form any sort of comprehensive picture. We knew one thing for sure, that my father was sixteen-years-old when the Germans invaded Latvia. He lived in apartment no. 11 in that big building with his parents, younger brother Reuven (Robby) and his older brother Ze'ev (Seew - Ze'eva). His aunts, uncles and cousins lived nearby. When the War ended in 1945, no one was left except for his father Samuel (Shmuel) and himself. They were the only ones who survived.

DID YOU READ WHAT I TOLD YOUR SON?
March 2006, Israel

In 2003, my eldest daughter Noa asked my father to tell her about his experience during the Holocaust for a school 'Family Roots' project. My father refused, as usual, and told her, "You do not need to know, it's not important." Three years later, when it was my son Itamar's turn to prepare the 'Family

Roots' project, he too wanted to ask my father about his experience. I told him the answer his elder sister had received and warned him that it was a subject that his grandfather never spoke about. "I'll try anyway, what have I got to lose?" replied Itamar, with the confidence of a thirteen-year-old boy who knows everything. Two days later, on a Friday evening, my father called me and said "Tell Itamar to come to me tomorrow, Saturday morning, with pens and paper. He will have lunch at our place."

Itamar stayed with his grandparents all of Saturday. He came home really late, exhausted, and went straight to bed without saying a word. That night the phone rang. I picked the phone up but before I could find out who the caller was, I heard my father asking, "Have you read what I dictated to your son?" as if he'd known in advance that I'd pick up the phone. When I answered that I hadn't, he answered briefly, "Then read," and the conversation was over.

I rushed to Itamar's room; he was asleep. He had a troubled expression on his face. On the desk beside his bed I saw the notepad that he'd taken to his grandfather. I hesitated for a moment. I knew that the notebook held the answers to the many questions I had been asking myself for years, and I wasn't sure I wanted to find out the answers; but, overcome by my curiosity, I picked up the notepad and before I could leave my sleeping son's room, I had already opened it up. For the first time, I was able to get a glimpse into the story of my father's life during the Holocaust from this densely handwritten manuscript.

I was in a state of a shock. What was written did not

match what we thought we knew at all. There was a totally different story altogether. My father was not even in Russia during the Holocaust, as we had thought, and towards the end of the War, he was transferred by sea from Latvia to Germany, where he stayed until the end of the War as a forced labor worker in a forced labor camp. The camp was part of the Stutthof concentration camp, one of the most notorious of all concentration camps. I couldn't sleep that night. Whenever I closed my eyes, more and more questions arose in my mind. It felt like I was holding just a small part of a big, tragic story, although I didn't yet know what it was.

The next day I spoke to my father. When I asked him for more details, he refused. "That is all and that's it," he said.

WHAT MORE DO YOU WANT TO KNOW?
July 2009, Israel

Three years went by and the subject was never brought up, until the death of my father's step-sister, Olga Brudnicki Rogalin, or as we used to call her, Auntie Olga. Olga was born in Latvia and although not my father's biological sister, had always been our Aunt. Her only daughter, Tsvia, is a close and beloved cousin to us, in every aspect! Aunt Olga and Dad had known each other from childhood and after the War, her mother and Samuel, my father's father, married, after they had both lost their spouses during the War.

During the thirty-day memorial service ('Shloshim') of Aunt Olga, my brother Assa and my father were walking slowly in the Holon cemetery paths from Olga's fresh grave to my grandfather Samuel's grave. Assa told my father about a book that I had given him, describing the Holocaust of the Jews of Latvia, which had left a great impression on him. "Dad", Assa approached my father and said, "After reading this book, I have many questions I want to ask you." My father replied simply, without any hesitation, "**So ask. What else would you like to know?**"

Assa had a few questions, I had many. I asked and asked, and we discovered what we had always suspected. **My father remembered everything. My father didn't have any memory problems**.

This is how the conversations with my father began in July 2009, and it continued for many months. I would go to my parents' house on a Saturday morning, sit on the balcony near the green garden, ask a few questions, but mainly listen, and write bullet points in my notebook.

Sometimes my father would stop speaking and refuse to continue. "It makes me too tired", he would say, "For years I have exerted so much effort trying to forget, it exhausts me to talk about it. Now, I cannot do it anymore" he would add, and go silent. After a while he would relent, and we would continue.

Sometimes, when I arrived early, I had to wait until my father had finished some of the chores he was working on, which he used to call 'Projects'. Once this was re-painting the white wooden fence which he had built with his own hands; another time it was repairing the wooden roof he had built himself over the parking lot at the entrance to the garden; another time it was building and hanging the wooden shelves in the living room. My father would sit on a chair on the porch wearing his gray work clothes, stained with color and covered in dust and wood chips. His passion to complete different 'Projects' using wood as a raw material, and his technical skills to do so, were a fertile ground for the many projects he had carried out at home for years.

GRANDFATHER SAMUEL GUTKIN HAS SOMETHING TO SAY, TOO...

At the same time that my father and I were having our conversations, I looked for information on the internet, from which I learned a lot about the Holocaust of the Jews in Latvia and specifically the Jews in Riga. For example, on a website called "The Jews of Latvia" (jewsoflatvia.com)[1] I discovered a book by Max Kaufman written as early as 1947. This book is very unique, as it was written soon after the actual events and includes a chilling description of the Holocaust of the Jews of Latvia[2].

One day, I decided to take a new direction. Instead of searching for information using the same keywords I'd been using, I used the Google search engine to look for information about my father's relatives from right before World War II. I used the name of the husband of Rachel (Rosa), my father's

---

1   http://www.jewsoflatvia.com/thebook.html.

2   **Churbn Lettland - The Destruction of the Jews of Latvia,** by Max Kaufmann (translated from the German by Laimdota Mazzarins).

cousin, who had a very uncommon name: Zalia Vazbuzky (Zalja Vazbucky).

The result was incredible and led to an unexpected chain of events: it caused my grandfather Samuel, who had died in 1967, 43 years earlier, to join my efforts in restoring the events and "to tell" his version regarding some of the events my father had spoken about. As strange as it may sound, this is what really happened.

One of the few results that surfaced from searching the name "Vazbuzky" using the Google search engine, was a book called "The 'Final Solution' in Riga: Exploitation and Destruction, 1941-1944", by the authors Andrej Angrick and Peter Klein. The book had been published in English in 2009 by the Berghahn Books publishing house.[3]

Much to my surprise, when I searched for the name 'Gutkin' in the online book, I found out that the book cites a statement multiple times given on 21.3.1963 by a man called Samuel Gutkin. According to one of the quotes, Vazbuzky had spoken to that Samuel Gutkin in the ghetto. 'This is not a coincidence', I thought to myself, 'It must be connected to my family'. I started reading all the citations where the name had been mentioned. In one of them, I found a nearly

---

3   The book "The 'Final Solution' in Riga: Exploitation and Annihilation, 1941-1944" was originally written in German by the authors Andrej Angrick and Peter Klein and published in Germany in 2006 by the Wissenschaftliche Buchgesellschaft publishing house in the city of Darmstadt. The book was translated into English in 2009 by Ray Brandon and published in 2009 by the Berghahn Books publishing house.

identical description to the story my father had told me about the circumstances of being expelled from their apartment in the big building shortly after the arrival of the Germans in Riga. Now I knew for sure that it was a statement given by my grandfather nearly fifty years ago; a statement that no one had known about.

It was obvious to me that I needed to make every effort to get my hands on that document. I had hoped that this document could shed light, from another perspective, on the story of his and my father's survival.

I approached the Yad Vashem institution in Jerusalem and inquired whether they had a statement that was dated 21.3.1963 from a man by the name of Samuel Gutkin. They came back with a negative response.

I decided to contact the original publisher of the book. Using Google again, I tracked down the original publisher's website and their email address to try to get in touch with them. I drafted an email in which I wrote that I am apparently the grandson of the same person mentioned in the book they have published, and asked them to help me contact the authors Angrick and Klein. I further explained that I wanted to contact the authors so that they could tell me where they had found the statement and how I could receive a copy of it. I waited expectantly for a few days, but nothing happened; there was no reply to my email.

I then decided to try my luck with the Berghahn publishing house. I began my journey using Google again and I tracked down the publishing house website and a list of email contact addresses, each with a different role in the organization in New York and Oxford. None of these roles included 'assisting people mentioned in a book published by the publishing house or their descendants'. I decided to take a gamble and I chose to contact Ms. Melissa Spinelli, whose name appeared on the list. I sent her the following email on May 25, 2010 at 12:35:

Dear Ms. Spinelli,

I recently found out about a book named "**The 'Final Solution' in Riga: Exploitation and Annihilation, 1941-1944**", written by Mr. Andrej Angrick and Mr. Peter Klein (translated from German by Ray Brandon), and published by Berghahn books.

This book mentions in numerous places a **Samuel Gutkin** from Riga and quotes from a statement that **Samuel Gutkin** gave on March 21, 1963 (in the English version, for example: page 71, page 91 footnote 76, page 120 footnote 5, as well as numerous other pages).

I am the grandson of (the late) **Samuel Gutkin** (I am the son of Max Gutkin, born in 1925 in Riga, who is the only son of the late Samuel Gutkin that survived the 'Final Solution' in Riga) and I would like to know where can I find a copy of the above-mentioned statement.

I would greatly appreciate your assistance in contacting Mr. Andrej Angrick and/or Mr. Peter Klein about this piece of information.

Thank you very much for your help.

Kind Regards,
Robby (Gutkin) Govrin

I waited for an answer and it did not take too long to arrive. After a few hours I received the following email from Ms. Spinelli:

Dear Robby

I would be happy to forward your email to Andrej Angrick and Peter Klein.

It is our policy not to give out the contact information of our authors without first checking with them. I will be in touch once I hear from them.

Best wishes,
Melissa

Her response indicated that I'd gambled well and that there was a good chance that I would eventually get in touch with the authors. I just had to wait. Throughout that week I checked my email again and again for an answer, but there was none.

Eventually, when I began to fear that maybe the issue has been forgotten, I received an astonishing email:

Dear Robby Govrin,

Ann Przyzycki from Berghahn Books recently informed me of your wish to find the statement of Samuel Gutkin's confession at the German court in Hamburg on March 21, 1963. It is correct that Mr. Angrick and I used his statement several times in our book concerning the 'Final Solution' in occupied Riga. Unfortunately, I'm not in possession of a copy of this single statement, but I think Mr. Angrick, who widely used this statement, had archived one.

Andrej Angrick is currently on vacation, but he should be back during the next few days. Perhaps it would be possible to fax this statement to you...it is a German text.

Samuel Gutkin's original confession from 21.3.1963 is now located at the Staatsarchiv, Hamburg, Germany. But I think you should wait until Andrej is back.

Best wishes from Berlin,
Peter Klein

It was a huge surprise. Not only did I finally make contact with Mr. Peter Klein, one of the authors of the book, and now had the email addresses of the two authors of the book, but I also found out where my grandfather's statement actually was. I sent him a warm 'thank you' email and waited for Mr. Andrej Angrick (the other author of the book) to return from his vacation.

On June 12, 2010 I could no longer wait. I emailed Mr. Andrej Angrick directly and asked if he could help me get a copy of my grandfather's statement. At the end of my email I added that I would be in Riga the following week with my brother Assa and that we would be staying at a hotel right across from the building mentioned in his book. I then suggested that he join us. I hoped that it would make him interested and increase the chance of him replying my email.

That same evening, I received his reply:

Dear Robby Govrin,

The easiest way for me to send you your grandfather's statement is by fax. Thank you very much for the invitation, but I am at a workshop in Paris from Sunday for one week. Maybe next time.

I hope that you have a good time in Berlin, and of course in Riga.

Best wishes,
Andrej Angrick

I knew now that it was only a matter of time until I'd find out what my grandfather could tell us. Five days later, during my stay in Riga, I received an email from Matthias Kamm, a friend of Andrej Angrick, which had a photocopy attached to it - a photocopy of a statement given so many years ago. I finally had the document.

I held the photocopy of the statement and felt tremendously excited. I didn't know what was written in it, why it was given and where, but I knew one thing for sure: Grandpa Samuel was aware from the skies above of his son's difficult journey to retrieve his memories of the Holocaust and again came to protect and help him, just as he did during the War. This time, he came to help me restore the story of their survival, or at least a part of it.

Immediately upon returning to Israel, I asked my friend, the Attorney Jul Bardos, to translate the statement from German.

It is now only natural for me to include Grandpa Samuel's story in this story, using parts that were mentioned in his statement. A statement returned from the ashes.

Only a thousand Jews, out of a population of ninety-five thousand Jews of Latvia, survived the Holocaust

When the German army invaded Riga, Latvian Jewry totaled at about 95,000 people (after thousands of Jews managed to escape to the Soviet Union and thousands more were killed trying to escape). The number of Latvian Jews who were lucky to remain alive at the end of the War was estimated at about 1,000 people, which is 1% of all Latvian Jewry before the War.

My father and Grandpa Samuel were amongst those 1,000 Jews who remained alive.

Why did my father survive the Holocaust while other members of his family did not? We can only speculate the answer. One can understand from his survival story that it was not a coincidence. My father probably survived because of the combination of his natural born technical and language skills and abilities gained as a child before the War, as well as the miraculous survival skills of his father Samuel. Above all, a lot of luck played a part in him surviving and enduring what happened to him during the Holocaust, which was beyond his control.

But there was another factor that played a role in rescuing Grandpa Samuel and my father; **the raw material: wood!** A raw material whose origin is the endless forests covering the land of Latvia, which was the cornerstone of one of the most important export industries in Latvia on the eve of World War II.

The vast knowledge, experience and expertise that Grandpa Samuel had when it came to using wood as a raw material and the production of wood products, was very special to him. They provided that added-value which, combined with luck, played a major role in contributing to the rescue of Grandpa Samuel and my father, and to the fact that they survived and remained alive.

CHAPTER ONE

CHILDHOOD - WELFARE, LANGUAGES AND UPHEAVALS
1925-1940

1925-1931

January 1925 had been a very cold month in Riga. My father told me it was so cold that my mother was ill with pertussis (whooping cough) and as a result, I was born already ill with the pertussis disease. I would choke from time to time, my face would turn blue and if I didn't get a pat on my back, I'd probably be dead. **My parents gave me the name Max.**

There was no cure for whooping cough at the time, and the treatment I received was from a city called Jurmala on the shores of the Baltic Sea, amongst pine trees and a salty wind wafting from the ocean. A chubby Russian nanny held me with a blanket outside the Dacha rented by my parents from morning until evening, even though the temperature outside was roughly -10 degrees Celsius.

It was cold, but it was successful. After six weeks of the treatment, I was cured of pertussis. In March 1925 we returned home to apartment no. 11 in the big building on 88 Brivibas Street in Riga.

I was not the eldest child. I had an older brother born in 1921; he was four years older than me. His name was Ze'ev (Wolf), but everyone called him Ze'eva. In 1929, when I was four-years-old, my younger brother Reuven was born and we all called him by the nickname Robby.

My father, born in 1890, was called Samuel (Shmuel) and my mother, born in 1895, was called Mania (Malka). During the years preceding my birth, my father had become a very successful secular Jewish businessman who was well acquainted with the evolving business community in Latvia.

Father owned a tree trunk processing plant called Zunde, which occupied a large area across the Daugava River.

Following the establishment of the independent state of Latvia after World War I, trees and wood products became Latvia's main export industry. The trees were logged, leaving tree trunks in the forests, cut and unused. These trunks interfered with the planting of new forests. My father made his fortune and built his business on the brilliant idea of purchasing state licenses at a low cost to cut and dispose of the trunks that were left over after being logged in state-owned forests.

Dad and his men would blow up the tree trunks, collect the logs that remained after the blast, tie them together with an arched wire one meter long so it would make a kind of thin iron hoop made out of 10 cm logs. My father and his employees would sell those hoops for heating purposes.

In 1923, Dad noticed a major boom in the building industry in Riga and predicted that the construction side would increase the demand for wooden boards. At the same time, he found out that a barbed wire manufacturing plant was for sale. The plant was located on the bank of a small part of the Daugava River called Zunde, hence the name of the plant. Dad sold the hoops business and with the money he purchased the plant and turned it into a boards and wooden crate factory. Dad would purchase logging permits of state-owned forests near the river during the winter. He would drag the logged trees over the ice to the river using horses, tie them up and stack them side by side. When spring came and the ice melted, he would go to the places where he stacked the trees, and sail the tied trees right to the plant's doorstep. Dad built a small railroad on the riverbank close to the plant, starting at the large storage yard entrance and ending in the river, about three feet below the river's water level. Iron carts would run on the track into the water and get loaded with logs, without having to lift them at all. After that, the horses would drag the carts to the big storage yard, where the logs were unloaded and left to dry for about two weeks. After being dried up, the logs were sawn lengthwise according to orders received for building boards.

The rest of the logs would go through the process of drying, industrial processing and would finally be used as raw materials in the wooden crates production line. Wooden crates were sold to everyone. The crates were used to manufacture beehives for the government, the production of soap boxes and other products and even exported to various countries, including Britain and Germany (ammunition crates for both the British army and the German army), and Palestine (boxes for packing oranges). On the riverside near the plant there was a dock where ships would unload the raw materials and load the factory-made products.

Wood residues would be cut for firewood for the enterprise itself, and were also sold as firewood for the apartments in Riga.

Over the years, Dad managed to purchase several real estate properties throughout Riga. Included in this was almost half of the big building on 88 Brivibas Street, which included about 70 apartments, multiple service areas, cellars, and shops at street level. As the owner of the largest share of the big building, Dad was accepted as the mover and shaker.

Our family lived in apartment no. 11, which had five large spacious rooms and some service rooms. My parents regularly employed a full-time housekeeper who also lived in the apartment along with the entire family, and helped my mother with the house chores.

In addition to my parents and my brothers, I also had aunts and uncles and many cousins, all of who lived in Riga and were in constant contact with us. Uncle Lyuba, my father's brother (he was three years older than Dad) looked like my father – big build, medium height and a round face. He always had a smile on his face, which made him my favorite uncle. He came to visit us at least three times a week, always with a smile. Mom used to say that Lyuba always brought along a joke and joy. Uncle Lyuba had a technical equipment warehouse in the center of the Riga market. As I liked dismantling and assembling engines and different objects that I found, I enjoyed going to the warehouse and asking him for some metal or wooden parts for my "projects" or searching for different tools that I needed. Whenever I needed one tool or another and asked Mom to get it for me, she would always ask me, "Why do you need it...?" and it was difficult to explain. On the other hand, when I asked Lyuba for a tool or a part, he never asked any questions, and immediately let me have it.

Until he died in 1938, when I was 13-years-old, I'd go to his warehouse and ask him for raw materials or tools I needed for my "projects". He would call one of his employees and ask him to help me find whatever I needed.

His wife, Aunt Fanny, was a fat and short woman, and had only one leg. The missing leg was amputated due to diabetes. Their eldest daughter, who was thirteen years older than me (she was born in 1912), was called Rosa (Rachel). After marrying an engineer named Zalia Vazbuzky, the owner of an aluminum pots producing factory in 14 Gogol Street (opposite the Great Synagogue of Riga), she moved to an apartment that was close to my school. Whenever I visited her she gave me a candy, so I used to visit her often on my way home from school. Uncle Lyuba and Aunt Fanny's son was born after Rosa and was named Ze'ev, like my brother; so as not to confuse between them, everybody called him Volya. He was nine years older than me (he was born in 1916) and didn't pay me much attention. Uncle Lyuba and Aunt Fanny's youngest son was Benjamin, but everyone called him Nyoma. He was only six years older than me (he was born in 1919) and didn't pay much attention to me when we were young, either. Everything changed after the Germans invaded Latvia, but I'll get to that later.

In addition to Uncle Lyuba, another one of my father's

brothers lived in Riga with his family. He was three years younger than Dad and his name was Boris. Physically, he resembled my father and Uncle Lyuba, but he was nothing like them in character. He was a religious man who always wore a hat and served as the collector (Gabay) of the Synagogue. He was always serious and never smiled. His wife was called Malka, like my mother. So as not to be confused, everyone called her Nina. They had two daughters, one a year older than me named Gena (Hiena) and the other was one year younger than me, called Rachel. I didn't have any contact with Rachel, but Gena and I were close, and when we met we would speak a lot amongst ourselves.

We also had a cousin named Tina, who was actually my father's cousin and was his age. She was a widow and had a business of manufacturing large size bras and corsets (like my Mom). I loved going to Tina's shop with my mom to peek at the women who were trying on bras. Tina had a daughter named Lucia (Lusja), who was the same age as my eldest brother, Ze'eva. She went to a school that was inside the Jewish Hospital "Bikur Holim", and after six years of studying she was trained to be a nurse. She used to come and visit us many times and was always very nice to me.

Taube Schalman, my mother's elder sister (she was older than Mom by eighteen years!) whom I knew as Aunt Ljuba, also lived with her family in Riga. Her husband was Naum (Nachum) and he was also a cousin of my father. This meant that they were our relatives both on my mother's and father's side, and they had four children. Abraham was the eldest, and everyone called him Riga because he smoked Papyri (a kind of cigarette) called 'Riga'. Then there was Nyura, Rita and Monya. Riga was older than me by at least ten years. He had already studied in Paris, spent all his money and returned to Riga. I had the best relationship with him. He taught me how to ride a bike and it was he who gave me answers to all sorts of questions I had that no one else knew or didn't want to spend the time getting me the answer. The Schalman family lived in the same building as Uncle Boris and his family.

The Schalman family was extremely rich. Every spring Uncle Naum would buy the future crop of large areas of Prussia and sell the actual crop in the Autumn. But in 1929, when I was four-years-old, the bank where Uncle Naum deposited all his money went bankrupt as part of the global economic crisis, and he lost his fortune. All he had left was a residential building and he could barely support his family on the rent he charged the tenants.

So I was surrounded by parents, siblings, aunts, uncles and many cousins my whole childhood. We got together with them regularly and routinely. All were professionals or business owners. Everyone made a good living and they all invested in their children's education, as did my parents.

From a young age we had a private tutor, Fraulein Martha. She was German and I remember her as a beautiful, tall and slim woman. I loved her very much. She only spoke German to my brothers and me. Dad told me years later that he and Mom chose a German tutor because German was the language that important people (aristocracy) in the city spoke. They themselves did not speak German, but because they spoke Yiddish they were able to understand. In addition, we had a maid who spoke Russian to us. So when I was four-years-old, I could speak two languages: Russian and German.

At age four I was sent to a kindergarten, which was on the sixth floor of one of the other entrances to the big building. Mom took me to the kindergarten only once, and from then onwards I would always go by myself as I already knew the way. I remember laughing at the kids whose parents had to accompany them to kindergarten. Most kindergarten children lived in the big building. Within a short while, the children who lived in the big building became my friends, and we would play together in the courtyard, which then seemed huge to us.

When I was six-years-old I was sent to the German school "Erich - German" where most of the students were Jews. The school was about half a mile away from our house and just like with the kindergarten, my mother accompanied me to school on day one, and after that I walked alone along Brivibas Street - from home to school and back. I studied at that school for three years, including preparing class, First Grade and Second Grade.

Ze'eva went to the Ezra Jewish School where he was taught in German, so Ze'eva, Robby and I spoke in German to each other, and Russian with Mom and Dad.

Whilst I attended the German school, Mom decided it was time to start using the grand piano sitting in the living room of our apartment. She organized a piano teacher who started teaching me music and how to play the piano. I had to practice for two hours each day and soon those music lessons and daily training became a nightmare. Mom insisted on the lessons and wouldn't give up, and we argued every day about how long I needed to practice. I took advantage of every opportunity I had to avoid playing and Mom would ask Uncle Boris from time to time whenever he would visit us, to explain to me, either in words or in "any other way", the importance and the need to practice playing the piano every day. Piano lessons were a source of constant dispute for years.

1932-1934

My cousin Nyura Schalman was sent to study in France like her brother, Riga, who lived in France a few years earlier. Monya, their younger brother, joined them and began studying Medicine. While staying in Paris, Nyura met her future husband, a Jew from Moldavia by the name of Lionya (Aryeh) who studied Medicine. They came to Riga on a visit, got married and then returned to Paris. It turned out that instead of learning, the young couple spent most of their time enjoying life. Unlike them, young Monya studied hard. Not surprisingly, Lionya failed his Medical exams and asked his talented young brother-in-law, Monya, to try and take the tests in his place. Monya agreed to do so and took the test under Lionya's identity. Unfortunately, they were caught and were immediately expelled from Medical School.

Having no choice, the three moved to live in Marseilles in southern France, where Monya registered again at the Medical School there (probably by changing the spelling of his last name). In 1932, Nyura and Lionya joined the French delegation to the first 'Maccabiah Games', which opened on

March 28, 1932 in Tel-Aviv, Palestine, and they did not return to France. Their daughter Nellie, my beloved cousin, was born in Israel.

1933

During the year 1933, when I was eight-years-old, my cousin Riga Schalman left us and immigrated to Palestine, much to my despair. He settled in Tel Aviv. As a Zionist family, we all viewed it in a positive light and I was actually jealous to some extent that he was fulfilling the Zionist vision.

1934 - 1935

On May 5, 1934 there was a political upheaval in Latvia. With the help of a militia of farmers, a Latvian nationalist named Janis Ulmanis scattered the government, got many of the members of Parliament arrested and established a dictatorship. One of the first laws set by the new government was to separate students based on their religion. The law also stated that a student who was not accepted to a school of his religion would be sent to a Latvian governmental school.

***

When I was nine-years-old a law was issued, after which the students in my school were dispersed to different schools according to their religion. The best Jewish students were accepted to Jewish schools and I, as a mid-level student, had no choice but to go to a Latvian school. My only problem was that I didn't know the Latvian language.

My parents found a solution; during the summer, before school started, they hired a Jewish student and reached an agreement with him in which he could live in our apartment, provided he spoke Latvian with me and my brothers and teach us, especially me, to read and write Latvian. His name was Isia (Israel) Schlossberg.

I have the best memories from when Isia lived with us. Isia was a 19 or 20-year-old young man in his first year at university. He had fair hair, a smiling face and was medium height. He was very talented. He had an amazing musical gift that enabled him to play melodies on the piano that he had only heard once before. But for me, his most impressive talent was his technical ability combined with what I called 'golden hands'.

When he received his first paycheck from my parents, he bought himself an old Royal Enfield motorcycle and immediately began overhauling it in the courtyard of the big building. I was his chief assistant. While my brothers showed little interest in the new vehicle, I felt that I had discovered an exciting new world. Isia would spread a blanket on the floor and put the different parts he dismantled from the motorcycle next to one another. My job was to clean each part and put it back in its place on top of the blanket and Isia would use the time to explain to me what the function and importance of each part of the motorcycle was. Every day I would anxiously wait to return home from school and sit with Isia in the courtyard to dismantle the motorcycle together.

Isia even promised me that he would take me for a ride on his motorcycle. He didn't just promise, he actually kept it. One day Isia called me and asked me, "Are you coming?" At first I didn't know what he meant, but he gave me a mysterious smile and finally said, "Are you coming with me to ride the motorcycle?" No one could possibly have been happier than I was in that moment. When we went down to the courtyard, I was skipping down the steps to get to the motorcycle as soon as possible. Isia sat me on the back chair, a sort of triangular chair that was attached to the motorcycle's body with two huge springs, and put my feet in place even though they were too short and couldn't reach the footrests. He explained me that I needed to put my hands around his body and hold his waist, and told me in a serious voice, "You have to hold me the whole time, do you understand?" I nodded my head excitedly, waiting with a great deal of vigilance for the trip to begin. I wasn't afraid, not even for a moment.

Isia easily moved his leg to the other side of the motorcycle and sat on the front seat. He set his foot back and pressed on the foot starter with force. The engine beneath us made a loud noise and I felt the motorcycle vibrate. I held Isia's waist so tight that I was afraid I was about to break his ribs. He turned to me and shouted over the noise of the engine "Are you ready?" I nodded my head and off we went. It was a long journey, at least for me. We drove to the city of Dvinsk (known today as Daugavpils) to visit his family, and returned back to Riga that same evening. It took us two hours in each direction. I concentrated the whole time; I never let go of his waist. The wind blowing in my face and the speed at which we passed the landscape made this trip one of the best experiences of my childhood.

I remember that when we got to Isia's house, he opened the door and we heard the charming melody of a piano. When I walked into the house I saw a piano in the living room that seemed huge to me, and an old woman sitting and playing it - Isia's mother. He explained that his mother was a piano teacher. I also met his sister Tanya, who was older than me.

During the months of summer our whole family moved to camp, the Dacha my parents hired each year in the Majori area in Jurmala, which was a strip of land stretching from the Baltic Sea shore to the route of the Lielupe River. Isia came with us. He taught me how to swim and sail a small sailboat that we had named 'Julie'.

Our next 'Project' was to build a small sailboat and sail it in the sea or the Lielupe River. I brought some wooden boards from my father's factory and together we built a meter-long boat that had two masts. We even sewed sails for the boat. After we completed the construction of the boat, Isia and I went on our first sail accompanied by Mom and Robby, who had made me promise I would allow him to sail the boat. I didn't want him to come, but Mom made me take him. I certainly didn't allow him to sail the boat before Isia and I had completed the operation successfully.

We reached the beach and Isia lifted the boat and opened the sails. The wind immediately blew them open and I was impatient to launch the boat in the water. But Isia very patiently cleaned the boat and finally raised it and began approaching the water. He was holding the boat high while

I was running next to him, and we both went into the water deeper and deeper until the water reached Isia's knees and my chest. It landed up being too deep for Robby, and we were left alone while five-year-old Robby stood grumbling behind us.

Finally, Isia put the boat in the water. I was afraid it might sink and I tried to hold it up, but Isia explained to me that we should let the boat get used to the water alone so that it would be able to handle water when we weren't near it, too. The boat got used to the water very quickly. In fact, the boat got used to the water too well, since the wind filled the sails and it began sailing into the sea without us. Isia began chasing it by swimming until he got to it. We were very lucky that he could swim fast.

Isia explained that that had happened because we didn't build a rudder nor an engine on the boat. The next morning he went to Riga with Dad by train and bought a record player in the flea market. He told me that instead of the engine spinning records, it would turn the propeller of a boat. We dismantled the engine of the record player together and Isia, with my help of course, put the engine into the boat, tied it at the back and after various measurements, drilled a hole in the back of the boat. He passed a very thin metal tube he had brought from town, connected it in a mysterious way to the engine and made it an axle. On the other side of the axle, he connected a small metal propeller (I have no idea where he had found it). Now the boat seemed more like a real boat to me. I was so tired that day that the next day Isia told me that while he was sealing the space between the axle and the body of the boat, I fell asleep while sitting right next to him.

The next day the boat sank right before our eyes, and it was probably from the water that came in from that exact hole.

I managed to overhaul my bicycle that summer with Isia's help. He had even taught me how to take pictures, develop the film and guided me on how to print the photographs.

That same year (1934) Aunt Ljuba and Uncle Naum decided to join their oldest son Riga who had immigrated to Palestine the year before. They got 'certificates' (permits to immigrate to Palestine during the British Mandate) as 'rich people' and went to live with their son in Tel Aviv. They opened a bakery on Herzl Street in Tel Aviv.

Summer vacation was over and on September of 1934 I began attending a Latvian school. This was a test on Isia's Latvian teaching skills. It was the first time I'd come face to face with the Latvian environment. There were eight of us Jewish children out of 34 children in my class, the rest being Latvians. One of the Jewish children was Max Michelson. He became my good friend, a friendship that successfully survived even the toughest tests that our brutal reality forced on us seven years later. Max Michelson remained a dear, good friend, even after the War, although we parted ways. He went to the U.S. and I went to Israel, and we keep in close contact until today.

In our first lesson we were seated in a classroom with four students sitting next to each other at a table for four. There were two tables in each row, so that in each row there were eight students.

After the students were seated in this class, it turned out that on the right end of the right quartet in my row Max

(Michelson) was seated and at the left end of the left quartet, another Max was sitting - me. When the teacher noticed this, she laughed and said that this is how she would remember our names: Max at each end. She also sat two Latvians named George on the left end of the right quartet and on the right end of the left quartet and was very pleased that she could remember the names of four students on her first day of teaching.

I didn't fit in to the Latvian environment at first. I found it very strange, but slowly improved my Latvian skills over time and was able to read and write Latvian better than the Latvians themselves. Isia had taught me well and it turned out that he'd done a good job.

Being with the Latvian children exposed me to sports activities in areas I hadn't know before; sports that were very popular with them: skiing, boxing, javelin throwing, discus throwing, hammer throwing, shot put and roller-skating. Every day, two hours were dedicated to sport lessons where we practiced the different sports. I really enjoyed the javelin throwing, but I loved the winter ski lessons most. Every Saturday morning we showed up at school, from which we'd traveled by tram to the Mežaparks, a posh area in the Northeastern part of Riga, taking our ski equipment with us - two bamboo sticks and two wooden skis, and we wore a standard tracksuit (training suits). After about an hour we would reach our training area, put the skis on and stand in a straight line in front of our sports teacher. The teacher began skiing and all of us, in a row one after another, would ski after him, careful not to deviate from the line for even a moment.

The teacher lead us up the hills and we would follow, he would ski downhill and we would follow. This went on for about two hours, until 12:00. Then we returned to school, returned the ski equipment to its place, and went home.

Since most of the Latvian youth belonged to the Scouts based on their area of residence, I decided to join the Scouts, too. The Scout group that I joined was a group of Jewish Latvian Scouts and its name was Troop 144. We would meet three times a week for two hours in the evening (at six or seven o'clock). We learned to do at least one good thing each day, we learned about the history of the Scouts, and we learned how to adapt to the field, set up a tent and work with ropes. Once a month we went out to practice what we had learnt. In winter we went on full-day ski trips, and a great camaraderie was formed among the members of the Troop.

During the summer of 1935 we went on Scout Camp for a month. The camp was far away from home and far from all transportation. Close to our camp was a Camp of joint Scouts from all over Scandinavia and Baltic countries, as well as England and Scotland. We patrolled and guarded our troop for an hour every night. This is how we became familiar with the night and its sounds.

One night I was awakened with the entire troop at two o'clock in the morning. The Troop Commander informed us aloud, "Everyone with sticks to the perimeter!" What had happened? The night guard, a 13-year-old Scout, woke up the troop commander and told him that the gate of our troop had 'gone for a stroll'. When he managed to convince the Troop Commander to get up to come and see the gate, it had already disappeared. The Troop Commander sent each of us in a different direction to look for the gate and see where it had gone. After half an hour everyone returned, but no one had found the gate, so we went back to sleep. At four o'clock in the morning a loud whistle pierced the air and we woke up again – this time it was our camp commander. We left our rooms, and to our surprise, we saw a fire in the center of the camp, our gate broken and burning within it. A group of Scottish Troop Scouts, dressed in Scottish skirts called kilts, were standing close by, looking very pleased with their success in surprising us. After the initial shock, we joined them and sang Scout songs until the morning – some great friendships were made.

That same year (1935), when I was ten-years-old, I started visiting Dad's factory, cycling there by myself on my bicycle. Dad wouldn't take me nor my brothers to his factory, but he didn't stop me from getting there myself. I would walk around in the different departments, enjoying looking at the big mills, ferries and carts moving the logs from the river into the drying area. I loved the smell of sawed wood that filled the air and the general atmosphere of the processing wood factory.

Most of all, I loved visiting the horses. The factory had six horses and six carts, used to take the firewood from the factory to sell in the city. The six carters (transporters) lived with their families in houses which were in the factory area, and on the side of each house there was a horse stable and livestock: a cow, a goat, a few sheep and chickens. When I came to visit the factory I would eventually reach one of the carters' houses and enjoy strolling among the farm animals.

During one trip I got to see the litter of a goat. I was so excited that I ran to Dad's office, burst straight in and, without waiting at all to find out what he was doing, I asked him to buy me a little goat. Dad was so shocked at my wild behavior that he just said "Okay". The next day, Dad went to one of the carters and bought me a goat. He took it to our Dacha in Majori, Jurmala. I loved playing with the little goat, although I'm not sure my Mom loved it so much because of the large mess it made. Unfortunately, the story with the goat didn't end well - At the end of summer, when returned to our apartment, we were unable to bring it along with us. As far as I know, Dad took it to the slaughterer and the goat's life ended on our dinner plates.

Sometimes, when I went to the factory, instead of playing with the carts or visiting the livestock, I would go on my bicycle or walk to a small airport called Spilve, which was about 2 kilometers away. There was a flight school and an Aviation Club there, amongst other things. At first, I would go just to look at the airplanes taking off and landing, and watch the aircrafts being serviced on the ground. After a while, the locals started asking me to hold some tools and help them out. Later on, they let me wash engine parts. Sometimes they even let me wash the actual airplanes! I was happy, and it gave me the feeling that I was grown up and that I was doing important things. I would spend many hours there. I actually outlined my future profession of many years to come with my own hands, but of course I didn't know that yet.

1936

During the year 1936 I left the Latvian school and went to study sixth grade at the Riga Hebrew Zionist City School. I was 11-years-old and had already mastered three languages: Russian, German and Latvian, but I didn't know Hebrew. My parents hired a rabbi who was a teacher in the same school to teach me Hebrew. He taught me how to read and write, as well as Hebrew reading comprehension. I remember my first lesson with him in which he taught me the Hebrew vowels including, 'Hirik', 'Pattah', 'Kamatz' 'Shva', 'Holam' and 'Shurouk'. By the time I was 13-years-old, I had already mastered both Hebrew and Yiddish.

The studies in the Hebrew school were at a much higher level than that of the Latvian school. As a result of that learning level, along with the difficulties in mastering the Hebrew language at that time, I was not one of the best students in my new class, and that's an understatement. Unfortunately, the educational program of the Hebrew school did not include subjects that I had really liked in the Latvian school: Gym and Sports.

The school supported Zionism and fulfillment in Israel and put a lot of social pressure on me to leave the Scouts, which I really liked, and to join the Beitar movement, which was founded at the end of 1923 (December 17, 1923) by Ze'ev Jabotinsky, in the city of Riga.

Sometime, probably in 1936, we were told that Jabotinsky was going to give a speech at the Jewish Club on 6 Skolas Street in Riga, and that we needed to protect him from attacks by Latvians or members of 'Hashomer Hatzair' (a Socialist-Zionist secular Jewish youth movement founded in 1913 in Austria-Hungary) or by party members of the 'Bund', the Jewish Communist Party. In those days there was a lot of tension between those groups and there was a serious concern that someone might attempt to disrupt Jabotinsky's speech. Tickets to his speech were sold and Dad, who was a Zionist, had also bought a ticket.

My brother Ze'eva was also a Zionist and volunteered to assist in managing the Beitar branch in Riga and in managing the Tel Hay Foundation. The Tel Hay was a foundation that raised and allocated funds to be used by Beitar. It was established to support the settlement of Jews in the land of Israel, military training and immigration to the land of Israel. The bulk of the moneys came from donations from its supporters. Ze'eva was assigned the task to distribute tin cans amongst Zionist Jews and Jewish institutions in Riga and then collect the full boxes and replace them with empty ones, much like the fundraiser boxes of Keren Kayemeth Le-Israel, the Jewish National Fund (JNF).

One evening at home, Dad told me that in 1929, delegates of the JNF came to Latvia and met with the Jewish leaders. In that meeting they asked the Latvian Jewish congregation to raise a total of one million pounds to finance the purchase of land in the Jezreel Valley in the land of Israel. And so it was that within that framework, my father donated a sum of seven thousand pounds, which was a huge amount in those days. Dad also told me that about a year later, the donors were informed that areas in the Jezreel Valley that had been purchased with their own money were registered in their names, and a lottery was held between the different donors to decide how the land would be divided amongst them. Dad said that he received ownership of over twelve dunams of land (one dunam equals 1,000 square meters), five of which were in a place called the Yokneam Hills, and the remainder in a flooded area in the Jezreel Valley, which was a swamp at that time. Years later, these areas were expropriated by the State of Israel for the paving of the Ramat David Airport runway.

Both in the Latvian school and in Beitar I encountered the growing trend of anti-Semitism for the first time. This was influenced by the rise of the Nazis in Germany and the impact of this on the Latvian population of German origin. About 10% of the Latvian population was of German origin and the majority of them sympathized with the Nazis. Many of them even became actual Nazis.

In the shop windows in Brivibas Street, in which I glanced every day when returning home from school, signs started to appear which read: "This is a Latvian store". One evening I heard Dad tell Mom and Ze'eva, that the University and the Technion announced that henceforth, the number of Jews to be admitted will not exceed 10%, just like the proportion of Jews in the total population of Latvia (they called it "numerous-clausus"). Dad said that as a result of this, a lot of the youth went to study professions like medicine, law, engineering and dentistry in the other European countries such as Czechoslovakia, Italy and Sweden. My elder brother Ze'eva tried to get accepted to the university, but despite his talent and high grades in high school, he was rejected because of the numerous-clausus rule. Having no choice, he went to work with Dad at the Zunde factory as an accounting apprentice.

The feeling that Latvia was no longer a safe place for the Jews as it once had been begun to grow. People started talking about immigrating to Palestine.

Dad and Mom had good friends, Zhenia and her husband Joseph (Osip) Rogalin, who lived in the port city of Liepāja (Libau) on the southwestern coast of Latvia where they owned a pharmacy. They had one daughter named Olga, who was my age, and I was quite friendly with her. Both families were well acquainted. Olga's and her mother's fate will be tangled with the fate of my father and mine, but in those days we didn't yet know what would occur.

In 1936 my cousin Rita Schalman married her fiancé, a medical student by the name of Aaron (Roma) Paperna. Roma was the brother of Zhenia Rogalin. After he finished his medical studies in Germany, he returned to Riga, but he and Rita immigrated to Palestine as he couldn't find a job in Latvia.

My cousin Rosa (Rachel) Vazbuzky also looked into the possibility of immigrating to Palestine. She traveled to Palestine alone, as a tourist, to investigate the option, but after she return she no longer raised the subject.

1937

Monya Schalman, the younger brother of Riga, Nyura and Rita (now Paperna) continued his medical studies in Marseille and completed them successfully. He immigrated to Israel in 1937.

In fact, upon his arrival in Palestine, all of Uncle Naum and Aunt Ljuba's family members lived in Palestine.

Monya Schalman started working in Tel Aviv and once a week he would volunteer a night shift in MDA (Magen David Adom). On one of those night shifts he met a beautiful nurse called Lea Fishbein, who had emigrated from Germany. They got married, and the lady who got the nickname 'Beautiful Aunty Leah' had now joined our family. They moved to Tiberias near the Sea of Galilee, where they lived for the rest of their lives and raised their two daughters, Dorit and Michal, my beloved cousins. Uncle Monya was the first chief doctor of the gynecology ward in the Poriya Hospital near Tiberias. He managed it for twenty-six years and has become a very famous person in the Jordan Valley. In recognition of his work, he got the honor to be buried in the Kineret Cemetery, not far from the grave of the famous local poet, Rachel.

1938

In January 1938 I turned 13-years-old. The preparations for my Bar Mitzvah began months in advance. As was customary in our family, Mom hired a 'Melamed' to teach me Judaism, reading and writing in Hebrew, how to read the Torah, how to sing the 'Maftir' and how to say the 'Brachot' (the blessings) at my ceremony. My teacher was a nice person from the Jewish religious school in Riga. Once, when he was supposed to come to my home to give me a lesson, he called in sick and asked if I would come to his house for the lesson instead. When I entered his house, I found out that he had two daughters my age and that their world was a completely different world from my own; they were both religious and I was secular, and we didn't have a common language.

In those days, it was customary for the Bar Mitzvah Boy to read a 'Drasha' (a sermon) by heart to his guests in German (or Russian) and in Hebrew. Mr. Herman Yadlovker, who was cantor of the Great Synagogue in Gogol Street (in front of Zalia Vazbuzky's factory), had written the text of the sermon in German, and my teacher translated the sermon into Hebrew. Herman was my Mother's cousin, and I knew him before this, of course. In the summer, when we moved to the Dacha in Jurmala, Herman would come to our Dacha with his kayak and offer my brothers and myself to sail with him. The first time I sailed with him I threw up a lot, but Herman promised that I'd get used to it. When I threw up the second time, I realized that I'd have to throw up many times before I'd get used to it, and I just stopped sailing with him on the kayak.

My Bar Mitzvah party was to take place in our apartment. On the evening of the event there was a large commotion in the house. Many chairs and tables were brought into the apartment, dishes with prepared food for the event also began to arrive and were put in the kitchen, and my mother tried to orchestrate all the tumult, with much difficulty. I was 'thrown out' of the house, so as not to interfere nor walk 'between the legs' and disturb.

In the morning, I was called to read the Torah in the Synagogue on Matisa Street, the Synagogue where my uncles used to pray. I did my portion of the prayer perfectly.

For the evening reception, Mom made me wear a white

shirt, a black suit and a black necktie, just like the grown-ups. Dad and Mom had invited more than one hundred guests; my aunts and uncles, cousins and friends of my parents who mostly belonged to Riga's secular Jewish business community, and many others. The guests sat at overcrowded tables, which were set in advance in our apartment, and were given a hearty meal.

At my mom's request I made a long speech, whose text was naturally approved by her in advance. After the main course, I stood up in the center of the apartment, and gave over the speech to all the guests.

After the guests went home and the cleaners raided the apartment and began their work, I asked Dad, "Why did you make me such a big Bar Mitzvah?" Dad looked at me seriously and answered, "Maxi, there are war clouds in the air and I don't know if we'll ever celebrate like that again." His answer really scared me, but I was too busy thinking about when I could start opening my presents.

In the summer we had a surprising visit! Aunt Ljuba and Uncle Naum announced that they were planning on coming to spend the summer in Latvia, to escape the harsh summer days in Palestine. Mom and Dad rented a Dacha for them in Jurmala at the Baltic Sea shore, not far away from our Dacha. When they arrived, it was a great joy. One evening, we all sat together and they told us about the good life in Tel Aviv, about Palestine, about their children and much more. They stayed with us for the whole of summer.

Summer had ended and Aunt Ljuba and Uncle Naum made

no preparations to return home to Palestine. When everyone started wondering why, we discovered that the picture they had described of their life in Palestine was very different from reality. It turned out that the family bakery in Tel Aviv was a failure; they had got into a lot of debt and decided to return to Riga for a short while to try and earn money to pay for the losses in Tel Aviv. But they didn't even have enough money to pay for their return to Tel Aviv. With my father's help they rented a small one-room apartment in Riga and lived at the expense of our family.

When they finally decided to return to Palestine, it was too late. Their decision to stay in Latvia for a short while had eventually cost them their lives.

1939

On August 23rd 1939 a Non-Aggression Treaty was signed between Nazi Germany, represented by German Foreign Minister Joachim von Ribbentrop, and the Soviet Union, represented by Foreign Minister Vyacheslav Molotov. That treaty determined, in a confidential section, the division of influence areas between those two states. It was further agreed in that treaty, among other issues, that Latvia shall be under the influence of the Soviet Union from that time onwards, and it established the division of Poland between Nazi Germany and the Soviet Union. The agreement was valid for a period of ten years.

On the first day of September 1939, Nazi Germany attacked Poland, invaded its territory and began conquering the German 'part' of Poland under the Ribbentrop-Molotov Treaty.

But even before those events, there had been much tension between Poland and Nazi Germany on the one hand, and between Poland and the Soviet Union on the other. As a result, Polish farmers who were usually employed in Latvian farmlands in the summer and fall, stopped coming. Therefore, on May 1939 the Latvian Ministry of Agriculture and the Latvian Ministry of Education in Latvia, published orders, by which students who didn't work for a month on the farms, would not be accepted to the next academic year in school.

***

Following the government order, Dad contacted one of his factory workers who had a farm twenty kilometers away from Riga and asked him whether I would be able to go work on his farm together with some of my friends. He agreed.

By mid-June we went to the farm. It was my cousin, Lyova Mirman, who was my age (his mother was my mother's cousin), his classmate Jascha Lieberman, and myself. Although the farm was twenty kilometers away from Riga, the three of us rode there on our bikes. Each of us loaded our bike with a tent and some clothes for a month. We stayed at the farm from mid-June till the end of July.

The job I was given by the farmer for the summer was as follows: every morning, after the cow was milked, I had to take it to a meeting point in the village where all the cows of the village were taken to a field to feed freely under a shepherd's supervision. In the evening, at about five o'clock,

I had to "welcome the cow" when it returned from the field, and get it back home. During the day, I had to remove weeds from the carrot or cucumber seedlings in the agricultural area of the farm. Twice a day we received a meal from the farmer: in the morning, after taking the cow to the field and in the evening, after I returned it and the milking was finished. My friends had other jobs: one had to clean the barn, the stable and pigsty; the other had to load the wagon with the manure that had accumulated in the barn, stable, pigsty and the rest of the farm and spread it in the fields.

One day Lyova and Jascha decided to try to ride a work-horse in the farm, and they called me to join them. Lyova and Jascha chose horses for themselves and succeeded in climbing and sitting on the horse on their first attempt. I, of course, was not so lucky. I climbed the horse, but he must have felt my insecurity and threw me off his back instantly. I flew into the air and landed on my butt, and I was very lucky not to get hurt. But I learnt my lesson, and I haven't tried to get on a horse ever since.

We spent the nights sleeping in the tents we had set up next to the farmer's house. At the end the month and a half, we got a certificate from the farmer confirming that we had worked in the village. We immediately rode to the Riga City Council to show that we had certificates and that we could go to school the next year. After that, each of us had to give the certificate to the school that we attended that same school year.

Although we didn't know it then, that school year, which began in the summer of 1939, was our last year at the Hebrew school.

Around the same time, the Russia-Finland war broke out. It was a sign that war was getting closer. It was pretty clear that the Russians would need a way out to the Baltic Sea through the ports of Latvia.

On the first day of September 1939, Nazi Germany attacked Poland, and thus began World War II. Soon rumors got to Riga about attacks against Jews in Poland by the Nazis. There was nothing new or surprising, as we had heard for some years now that the Germans had been persecuting the Jews in Germany. Anyway, these were still only rumors.

After the signing of the Ribbentrop-Molotov Treaty, and after the German invasion of Poland, the German government issued a demand addressed to all people of German origin in Eastern Europe, requesting them to leave their homes and immigrate to the newly German occupied territories in Poland. The message has also reached us in Latvia, Estonia and Lithuania, too. The local Hitler-Jugend, which was very active, started approaching all Latvians of a German origin and threatening to burn their houses down if they didn't immigrate to Poland. These threats were made publicly and personally, and the burning down of a significant number of 'refuter's' houses had their effect. Many Latvians of German origin immigrated to Poland. One night during dinner, Dad told us that his secretary who was of German origin had left, and one of the engineers at the factory had left Latvia, too. The German school, which was close to our school, emptied of students and was closed. Children of German origin who studied with us at the school didn't come to school anymore. Even families who lived with us in the big building began leaving. Children that I used to play with in the courtyard in the afternoon just disappeared. But the highlight was when Fraulein Martha, who had been mine and my brothers' nanny for many years, came to our home one night and said, with tears, that despite her reluctance, she was forced to leave Latvia and had come to say goodbye.

Within a few weeks it seemed that all the 'Germans' in Latvia had left.

On the other hand, soldiers dressed in the Red Army Navy uniforms started to be seen in the streets of Riga, probably as a result of the right of access to the Baltic Sea through the Baltic States including Latvia, given to Russia under the Ribbentrop-Molotov treaty. We, the children, identified these soldiers immediately by their beige uniforms and the epaulettes on their shoulders. We associated the appearance of soldiers in the streets with the news in the newspaper about a number of warships which had entered the port of Riga, and that the public had been invited to visit them. Our curiosity wouldn't allow us to remain indifferent to such an event, and a number of my friends from the big building and I walked towards the harbor. We arrived at one of the ships and joined the queue of visitors. I remember that we visited the different parts of the ship, and it was a great experience for all of us.

But, for many Jews, it was a sign of Russia's intent to invade Latvia. Following this, many Jews started leaving Latvia through Sweden and other ways. Twice, we ran away from school to accompany a girl from our class who left Latvia with her family. In one case we, the class, decided to walk up to the Riga Airport, a distance of nine kilometers from school, to say goodbye to one of the girls in class whose family immigrated to the United States via Sweden. We didn't ask any questions and we didn't inform anyone at the school; the whole class just went along for the walk to the airport and back. But the price was heavy. Upon our return, our teacher assembled us in class and yelled at us, "There are many spies in the city and you disappear without telling anyone about it! I will now start counting, and every fifth child will be suspended from school." Of course, my luck was to be among those suspended.

Suspended with me were my friends Alexander (Sasha) Cannes and Mark Israeli. My friend until today, Ruth Shomer, stood up and told the teacher that it was unfair and that it was the school that was at fault as the school should have organized a going-away ceremony for the departing student. Our teacher yelled back at her to sit down and shut up, or he would suspend her as well. I think that what saved her was the fact that she was a good student and the teacher knew it.

I went home and told Mom that there was a disease at school and it had been closed until further notice. She actually believed me. After five days at home, the school summoned all the parents of the students who were suspended from school for a meeting. Apparently, only then did the parents find out the true story behind their children staying at home. The rumor was that each parent had to pay 'a fine' as a condition for the return of his child to study in school, but when I asked Mom about it a few days later, when everyone calmed down, she denied it.

Malka (Mania) Gutkin in her youth

Little Max Gutkin with his mother Malka (Mania) Gutkin

From left to right: Max, Robby and Ze'eva Gutkin

From left to right: Malka (Mania), Ze'eva and Samuel Gutkin

Max Gutkin gives his bar mitzvah sermon

The big building on 88 Brivibas Street before World War II

The big building on 88 Brivibas Street in 1993

The Zunde Factory

CHAPTER TWO

IN THE SHADOW OF THE RUSSIAN OCCUPATION
1940

On June 17, 1940 the Red Army invaded Latvia and occupied it. The next day, the Red Army 'organized' the Latvian peoples' consent to become a state within the Soviet Union. Among the laws that were issued subsequently was a law to arrest whoever had anything to do with Zionism and stop all Zionist or Jewish activities.

June 17, 1940

For me, June 17 1940 started as a perfectly normal day. Completely by coincidence, I happened to be close to the main railway station of Riga when I heard the noise of a crowd of people who had gathered around the plaza opposite the train station. I approached and passed through the people until I got right to the front of the crowd. Then I saw three Russian tanks before me, with a big red flag fluttering over them. The crowd roared around me, cheering support for communism and for the Soviet Union. I learned that the Soviet Union had invaded Latvia.

Towards the afternoon, one could already hear heavy traffic in the streets. My mother pulled down the curtains of all the windows in the apartment facing Brivibas Street so that no one could see inside the apartment. But when I pulled the curtain aside from one of the windows and looked toward the street, I saw a long convoy of military trucks. There was no need to tell me anything; those were Russian army trucks. It became very clear to me that our lives were going to change.

When I told my mother what I had seen in the window, I saw the faces of my father, my mother and Ze'eva; they were all very worried. They looked at me, and Ze'eva told me very seriously, "Don't talk. Just do not talk." That's what I was told again and again, and that was also the atmosphere everywhere. Adults' faces were serious all the time, and no one spoke anywhere; everyone just stopped talking.

A few days later I learned that the Russians had organized a conference of the "Workers of Latvia" who 'requested' the Soviet to annex Latvia to the Soviet Union and it 'responded to the request'. From being citizens of a free and independent country, we had become subjects of the frightening Soviet Union.

On one of the following evenings, I heard my father tell my mother that the Russian occupiers had started to deport the city's wealthy citizens from Riga, including many of their friends, together with their families. From the names that my father had mentioned, it appeared that most of their friends had been deported. My mother was horrified and her face turned pale, but my father told her that he would take care of everything and that all would be fine. I don't know if it calmed her, but it reassured me. I trusted my father.

Indeed, in those days, the Russians deported thousands of people to Russia, 5,000 of which were Jewish (wealthy people,

Zionists, heads of families); many of them close friends of my parents.

Only much later did I learn what my father had done. My father, who was street-wise and had an incredible survival instinct, did not stay stagnant and after he had found out about the signing of the Ribbentrop-Molotov Treaty, he started working to ensure his survival. He created fictitious registrations in the various authorities by which he transferred ownership of the Zunde factory to a private share company and transferred the shares to Latvian owners who didn't know anything about it at all. For example, he transferred part of the shares of the factory to the drunken courtier of the big building. In retrospect, I remember that he did so, because he asked me to take some documents to be signed by the courtier. At that time, he had told me that it had to do with the actions related to the factory and nothing more. In this way he obscured the connection between his property and the family, and the family remained united in Riga.

The Russians located the city's wealthy people through the phonebooks. Next to each number published in the phonebooks, the name and position of the line holder was noted. After my father transferred the ownership of the factory to the share company, the description next to his name in the phonebook was changed and instead of it saying 'factory owner', it was noted that he was the manager of the factory, which meant that he was not one of its owners. That's what saved us from the Russians, but doomed our fate later on to fall into the hands of the Nazis and their Latvian collaborators.

But we couldn't escape the confiscation waves. One evening, there was a knock at the apartment's door. Ze'eva opened the door and at the doorway stood an officer and three soldiers in Red Army uniforms. Ze'eva backed away and immediately called my mother, who came to find out what the problem was. The officer pulled out a sheet of paper and read something in Russian. The noise caught my attention and I left my room in a hurry. I arrived just as the officer finished reading his announcement that they were confiscating our expensive grand piano that stood in the living room, and that they would come to take it the next day. When he left the apartment, my mother began to cry. The next day, that same officer and three Russian soldiers came back, entered the apartment and went straight to the family room where the piano was standing. My mother clapped her hands together and had a look of fear and utter helplessness in her eyes. My father wasn't at home, and Ze'eva also stood silently next to my mother. I actually wasn't afraid and I asked the officer who passed me by following the soldiers, "Why are you taking our piano away?" He looked at me for a moment, top down and shrugged, as if he didn't know what to say. The three Russian soldiers approached the piano, dismantled its legs, picked it up with a lot of effort and left the apartment with it. The officer left right after them and slammed the door shut behind him, without looking back even for a second. I was pleased because I realized that at last I was saved from the piano lessons I hated so much, and from having to practice playing the piano every day.

My father's factory was nationalized and he had lost his job. My brother Ze'eva once again failed to be accepted into the university. This time, not because he was a Jew, but because he was considered wealthy. He was also fired from my father's factory.

Our family's economic state worsened. My parents didn't have any source of income to support us. Having no choice, they started, together with a few friends, to make shoes with wooden soles. My father took care of preparing the wooden sole, Mr. Schlesinger who was a shoemaker by trade, prepared the shoe leather that was connected to the wooden sole together with my mother, and Mrs. Schlesinger sold the shoes using her old business connections. My brother Ze'eva also went to work. Since all this was not enough to survive, my parents began selling the property we had in order to raise money.

My parents also started renting out rooms in our apartment. The Russians had allocated only nine square meters per person, but we had a problem. Because we had been rich, we had such a large apartment where almost every room had an area of at least forty square meters. In the end, my younger brother Robby, my elder brother Ze'eva and I were left in one room, my father and mother had their own room and we also had the dining room left, which served as a shoemaking workshop.

Ze'eva was 19-years-old and was not at home most of the day. Most days and evenings he would meet with his peers, specifically with girls. I wasn't in our room most of the day because of my many 'businesses'; so little Robby used the room most of the day. In the evening, I'd join him in the room and Ze'eva would arrive very late. The result being that we did not really suffer from the room being overcrowded.

I was 15-years-old and I experienced a complete change

in my life. In addition to the huge change in my family's situation, life has changed beyond recognition for me, too. My school, the Hebrew school, was naturally closed and instead a communist Yiddish school was opened. As a Zionist, I couldn't stand the old-fashioned Yiddish Studies. I had to leave the school and move to a Russian evening school classes called Sabiedriska, where most of the students were Jewish. This is where I met with an old friend called Fima Feldhuhn who was older than me, but because he had polio he had studied with me in the past and now joined me in this school, too. After six months, I moved to a Latvian evening school in Raiņa Street. Fima Feldhuhn moved to this school with me, too.

I started working in a factory that built train cars in the mornings which was located down Brivibas Street, about four kilometers from home. Zalia Vazbuzky, the husband of Rachel (Rosa), my father's cousin, found this job for me. I was the assistant to an engine driver. My main task was to feed coal into the furnace all day and keep it running at a temperature of 80 degrees. After a while I also learned to drive an engine myself and occasionally, the engine driver allowed me to drive it. In the afternoon I returned home exhausted, covered with black soot that had fallen from the coal. I showered and went to study in school from six in the evening until ten o'clock at night.

Aunt Ljuba and Uncle Naum suddenly found themselves in territory under Soviet control and could no longer return to Palestine, although they really wanted to do so. My father found it difficult to finance their stay in Latvia and they had to support their life in Latvia mostly on their own.

CHAPTER THREE

GERMAN OCCUPATION
AND DEPORTATION TO THE GHETTO

1941

On June 14th ,1941, the Soviet police rounded up most of the city's wealthy citizens who were remaining after the deportation the year before, and all the former leaders of Zionist organizations and their families. In total, it was about 3,500 people from the city of Riga alone.

The next morning they were all sent to Siberia. The men were sent to labor camps after being separated from their families, and the rest of the family members were sent to other places in Siberia, without any paternal support or care. Most of the men died there within a year. Some of the other family members survived.

June 15, 1941

My friend, Fima Feldhuhn, didn't come to school. When I told my father, he said that the Russians had taken Fima and his family, and no one knew to where.

We often asked ourselves why a particular family was

taken while another family was not. We obviously didn't have an answer.

June 22, 1941

Eight days later, on June 22nd in 1941 the Nazi German army invaded the Soviet Union territory without prior notice, in violation of the Ribbentrop - Molotov Treaty. A few days later, the German army arrived in Latvia and on the first day of July 1941 they entered Riga. Many Jews tried to escape to the Soviet Union that day. About 5,000 of them were killed trying to escape and about 15,000 managed to reach the Soviet Union. Immediately after the Nazis entered Latvian territory, they started systematically killing the Jews who lived in the provinces and the rural areas outside Riga by shooting and then utilizing mass burial pits. Thirty thousand Jews were murdered by October 1941. Among the first to be murdered were the Jews of Libau (Liepāja); among them was Joseph (Osip), the father of the Rogalin family - Olga's father.

July 1941 - August 1941

Everything I described earlier about the events we had experienced so far turned out to be a children's game compared to what happened over the next few weeks.

On the morning of June 27th 1941, when the Germans entered the city of Libau, I was on my way to work like every morning. While on my way, I met a woman whose name I do not remember, who told me in a very serious tone, "Max, leave everything and go home immediately and stay there." I didn't understand what had happened and asked her, "Why?" but she wouldn't answer and began walking away, leaving me both surprised and greatly alarmed. I ran all the way home.

The next day we found out that the factory managers had given an order to connect all the engines and cars that were in the factory and load the entire factory's equipment on them. Then they ordered all the workers who were in the factory, each and every one of them, to board the cars. The train traveled toward the Russian border, crossed it safely and disappeared in Russia, together with all the passengers and the equipment that was loaded on it. If I had come to work that morning, I probably would have found myself on that train, too.

On Tuesday, July 1st 1941, the Germans arrived in Riga. That night, at around ten o'clock, we heard a loud banging on the back door of the apartment, the one that had a staircase going down to the inner courtyard. My father, who was still dressed, went to the door and opened it. Blumberges was standing in front of him, his face very pale.

Blumberges was a Latvian who operated a mechanical workshop in the internal courtyard, which he rented from the Internal Committee of the big building. He was often drunk and, in addition, he was late with his rent payments from time to time. My father even considered ending the lease contract and driving him out from the inner courtyard area. But Blumberges's wife begged my father to have mercy on her husband and allow him to pay the rent later. My father had agreed to her requests time and again.

My father quickly let Blumberges into the apartment and Ze'eva and I joined them to hear what he had to say. Robby was already asleep and my mother stayed in her bedroom. Blumberges entered and with a trembling voice told my father, "Everyone knew it was only a matter of time before these Germans arrived in Riga. The Perkonkrust's[4] had prepared for the Germans' arrival to Riga. Using the phonebook, they prepared a list of all the important and wealthy Jews in Riga whom the Russians hadn't sent to Siberia, but were on their list because they had a phone number. Today at noon, those bandits had already gone to the homes of all those people on the list. They took more than eight hundred Jews. They're bringing them into the police station courtyard next to the train station. People say that they have already begun shooting them. It's just a matter of time before they reach you. You and your older children, Ze'eva and Max, have to get out of here immediately."

Before I could understand the meaning of Blumberges's message, my father had already told Ze'eva and me to wait at the door, as we were. He ran into the bedroom and told my mother, who stood at the entrance of the bedroom and had probably heard it all, that he's taking us down to the basement. He started going down the back stairs to the basement quickly, where the heating facilities were. In the basement there was a

---

4   Members of the "Thunder Cross" (Pērkonkrust) - a Latvian ultra-nationalist and anti-Semitic political party that collaborated with the Nazi Germany forces in perpetrating the extermination of Jews in Latvia (Wikipedia).

little light and a number of old armchairs that someone had left there instead of throwing them in the trash. We sat there silently. I tried to ask something once, but Ze'eva silenced me and told me not to talk, as usual.

We hid in the basement until one o'clock in the morning, when we heard my mother calling us to come out. My mother and father hugged and my mother told my father that about an hour after we had gone down to the basement, there was a knock on the front door of our apartment and when she opened the door, she was pushed rudely aside and a group of 'Thunder Cross" men with swastikas on their sleeve entered the apartment. They searched all the rooms without paying any attention to her. When they couldn't find my father, they started interrogating her, shouting, on my father' and Ze'eva's whereabouts, and waking up little Robby in the process. My mother said that she told them that the Soviets took us on June 14th and sent us to Siberia and that she was left alone in the apartment with her little son. My mother also said that after a few minutes they had decided to leave it at that and left the apartment.

We went up to the apartment and went to sleep. In the morning I got up with everyone and we stayed at home, as if nothing had happened that night, as if one could erase yesterday's drama.

The next day, we found out about another atrocity committed by the Germans and their Latvian collaborators that night. A group of hundreds of Jewish refugees from Poland and Germany, who had arrived in Riga a few days before on their flight from the Germans, were housed at the Great

Synagogue in Gogol Street, right in front of Zalia Vazbuzky's factory. The Germans had found out about it from the Perkonkrusts and they were quick to surround the Synagogue from every side. After making sure that all the Jews were in the Synagogue, they locked the doors from the outside and set fire to the building and its poor temporary occupants. One could hear the cries of the burning people from far away, but no one dared to get close and confront the Germans and the Perkonkrusts who were rioting in an unleashed lust of power. Until today, the remains of that Synagogue stand as a silent testimony of that horror.

Grandpa Samuel tells us:

On the night between the 1st and 2nd of July, the citizens were called, through radio broadcasts, to report to their work on the 2nd of July. On the 2nd of July 1941, six thousand Jews were arrested in Riga. Those arrested were mostly intellectuals such as doctors, lawyers, factory owners, teachers, etc. Latvian policemen and Latvian citizens made the arrests. The prisoners had been detained for three weeks in the Riga jail and were then shot in the prison yard and buried. Out of about 6,000 detainees, 40 Jewish doctors were released, and all the rest were shot. During the victims' shooting, German officers were already running the Latvian police and the execution itself was carried out by an order of the Germans. I found out about the prison executions from Latvian police officers that I knew well before the war. A police officer named Bersins, with the rank of a Captain from the Riga Police, who had been stationed and active in the fourth quarter of Riga, had told me the details of the executions. I don't remember the names of the German officers who conducted this, I just know that they were SS members.

After the action I had described, all the other Jewish adults were taken to work in forced labor camps. During work, the German functionaries and the Latvians would behave crudely and violently towards the Jews and sometimes even kill them. I know, for example, that 50% of the Jewish forced laborers who were employed in the rehabilitation and rebuilding of the new bridge over the Daugava, were pushed to the river to their death by the German and Latvian guards. The Germans performed the arrests and executions of Jews by shooting routinely. I estimate that during one month in the first period of the German occupation, a number of between 10,000 - 12,000 people were murdered.

Uncle Boris did not return home that night. Aunt Nina told my father the next day and he went looking for him the next morning. My father was out the whole day, but when he returned, he gave my mother an update that Uncle Boris had died. He had been beaten the day before by passersby in the street and died. Just like that. Just because he was Jewish. My mother went into the bedroom and I heard her crying. Although I wasn't really fond of my Uncle Boris, who was always tough and serious, I couldn't stop thinking about my cousins Gena and Rachel, who were now left without a father.

In the days to follow, we all realized and formed in our hearts the recognition that sooner or later, we wouldn't be able to escape our fate and might need to run away. We tried not to leave the house at all and if it was necessary to leave, only at night. That way, we were able to avoid the harassments, arrests and killings of Jews that took place in the streets of Riga at that time. My father began discretely selling everything he could sell and buying golden coins with the money. My father had also managed to sell the stock of all the shoes that were left in the apartment to two Latvian women. One evening I saw my father peeling off the wallpaper in one of the corners of the apartment walls, removing the brick that became exposed under the wallpaper with a screwdriver. After removing the brick, he pulled out another brick. In the space created, my father hid a small box, put one brick back in its place and put the wallpaper back to normal.

Much later, my father told me that in the space created in the wall, he hid golden coins, a few family photos and all kinds of my mother's jewelry: a diamond bracelet, diamond earrings and a precious inlaid diamond watch.

At the same time, my mother began buying food that was suitable for long storage. She went to the market on Matisa Street, not far from home, even though food prices had gone up considerably since the German occupation and it was difficult to get such merchandise.

During the days following the night we hid in the basement, nothing new took place. But the persecution of Jews in Riga continued vigorously. Many were imprisoned, beaten or simply killed on the street by the Perkonkrusts.

Two weeks later, on July 15th 1941, at four o'clock in the afternoon, there was a knock on the apartment's main entrance door. We've learned to fear those knocks, but there was no choice but to open the door. At the entrance to the apartment stood a German officer wearing a gray uniform with red stripes on the sides of his trousers. It was clear from his uniforms and the insignia that he was wearing that he was a high-ranking officer. Two other people accompanied him - one was wearing a brown uniform with a red sleeve badge bearing the terribly frightening Swastika sign, and the other was a German soldier without an officer's rank. Without a word, the German officer gave a sign with his hand to his escort and they began searching the apartment, while we - Father, Mother who was holding Robby's hand, Ze'eva and I - stood at the side without saying a word.

At the end of the search, which lasted a few minutes, the soldier wearing the brown uniform approached my father and told him in German in a terribly quiet voice that our apartment was confiscated for the benefit of the German army and he himself was the commander of the "Latvian" district, neither more nor less. He told my father that our family had only fifteen minutes to 'disappear from the apartment, and that we had to leave all of its contents behind, in the same state that it was right then. He allowed us to take only one towel and a bar of soap with us, for each family member.

Grandpa Samuel tells us:

When I asked him for a written order in that regard, the man with the brown uniform answered that he was the regional commissar of Riga and that his verbal order was enough.

Then, without another word, the senior German officer together with the brown-uniformed man left the apartment, leaving the soldier who came with them at the front door to make sure that we take anything with us.

Compared to the grim officer and the frightening looking person wearing the brown uniform, the soldier who stayed in the apartment looked quite nice. He stood at the front door and after a few minutes he started shifting his weight from one leg to the other, almost swaying. My father noticed, and motioned me to help him with something in the bedroom. When I got close to him he told me to keep the soldier busy so he could not see what my father was doing. I walked up to the soldier and offered him a chair to sit down. He agreed to my proposal and sat down. Without another word, I placed a chair beside him and I sat on another chair blocking his line of sight toward the interior of the apartment. On the chair between us, I put a chessboard and offered him, in German, to play with me. The soldier smiled and asked me if I was sure I could play with him, and I said in all seriousness, "Yes". We started playing chess.

My father and Ze'eva used the time to take out all the valuables that were left at home: silverware, precious photographs, expensive fabric curtains, etc. They moved everything through the back door and the back staircase to Blumberges' workshop. My father found Blumberges there, gave him an update about what had happened and asked him to keep the valuables for us until we came back. Meanwhile, my mother was busy packing clothes for us in small bags which I think had already been prepared in advance in anticipation for this event. Beneath the clothes she hid some sheets and blankets, and food for one day. We left the house a short while after. We never returned to live in our apartment in the big building after that.

We walked along Brivibas Street toward Aunt Fanny's home, Uncle Lyuba's widow. My father, Ze'eva and I carried the bags we had packed and Mother held Robby's hand. We were all quite shocked by what had happened to us. No matter how prepared you are for such an event - and we were expecting troubles to fall upon us - when it happens, it hits you with such a force that it's very difficult to recover. My parents looked as if their world had fallen apart. Looking at Ze'eva's face, you couldn't tell a thing and for me, it was the saddest walk of my life. I looked at the floor and followed my father. About twenty minutes later we arrived at Aunt Fanny's apartment. My father knocked on the door and for a moment it seemed like no one was home. I could actually feel the momentary anxiety that passed through the bodies of my parents. At last, the door opened and Aunt Fanny's head peeked out. When she saw us, her eyes widened with concern. My father opened the door and went inside, and we immediately followed suit. Volya and Nyoma, my cousins, were also in the apartment. Nyoma went to Ze'eva, took the suitcase and put it aside. Volya followed and took the suitcase my father was holding.

Although I visited Aunt Fanny's apartment many times and knew it quite well, this time I felt like a complete stranger for the first time. I wanted to go home, but I knew that wasn't possible and I didn't feel at home at all. I sat down at the table in the living room and let my head drop. I just wanted to lie on a bed and go to sleep so this nightmare would be over. My father took Aunt Fanny aside and told her what had happened that afternoon. I didn't hear what was said between them but when they came back it was clear that Aunt Fanny had been crying. My father told me later that Aunt Fanny had told him that when the Germans came to Riga and began collecting all the wealthy Jews, her daughter Rosa and her husband Vazbuzky were very frightened, especially for the fate of their baby girl, Lena. Rosa and her husband asked Lena's Russian nanny to take baby Lena with her and get out of town. And so she did. Two weeks had gone by and there was no news from them. Since then and until today, Lena's whereabouts have been a mystery; my family had lost Lena forever.

I got used to the new situation very quickly. I was given a corner in the apartment to sleep in and it suited me just fine.

In the following days we stayed in the apartment and didn't leave. I remember that Volya played a lot of checkers with me. I also remember that my father needed clothes, and as he had the same build as his older, deceased brother Lyuba, Aunt Fanny gave him some of Uncle Lyuba's clothes that he wore.

A week after moving into Aunt Fanny's home, different laws against the Jews were issued. On July 25th 1941, all the Jews in Riga were required to register at one of the government offices. Three days later, a decree according to which all Jews had to wear a yellow badge was passed. Only a few days had passed when another ordinance came out concerning the prohibition of the use of public transportation by the Jews, a ban on the presence of Jews in public places (schools, too) and even a ban on Jews walking on the sidewalks. I think that the ban of walking on the sidewalk was the most difficult for me. Of all the laws, that ordinance made me feel very humiliated. I felt like a chokehold was slowly being tightened around us, but I knew I had my mother, my father and Ze'eva to protect me and that really reassured me.

September 1941 - October 1941

At the beginning of September 1941 I heard my parents discussing that on August 25th 1941 a new order had been issued, under which all Jews (that meant us too) had to move to the area of Maskavas in Riga, an area that had been be assigned specifically for Jewish quarters, before October 25th. This was known as the ghetto. The place designated for the ghetto area was not large, only a few blocks that had been mostly populated by Jews even before it was announced as the ghetto, but non-Jews lived there too, so they had to leave. The Jews who moved to the non-Jewish houses had to pay rent to the owners. The area was not in the city center and was certainly not a posh area; about 20 minutes' walk from downtown.

There was no order or organization in the transition of the Jews to the ghetto. It was every man for himself. Father went to the ghetto area to gather some information and found himself in Little Kalno (Maza Kalna) Street, a short street a couple of hundreds of meters long. At the upper end of the street stood a Pravoslav Church with three turrets, each headed with a kind of a dark onion-shaped crown. Old wooden houses, one or two stories high, stood on both sides down the street. Eventually, he rented a small wooden house with one floor and two rooms. The house had seen better days. The green color had started peeling from its broken walls and the spaces between the wall beams were clearly visible. There was an entrance door in the front in a rotten frame and on each side of the front door there were two large windows, sealed with dirty windowpanes that one couldn't see anything through. The roof was made out of metal slabs, brown from the rust, with broken metal gutters at the sides.

A few days later our family, Aunt Fanny and her two sons and Uncle Boris's widow, Aunt Nina, as well as their daughters, Gena and Rachel, moved in to the wooden house. All together a total of 11 people was crammed into those two rooms and slept on the floor.

At that time we didn't know that the Jews of Libau hadn't even been given the option to move to the ghetto and that their systematic murder had already begun.

December 2009

Assa and I visited Riga on December 2009. We decided to try and visit the different waypoints of the survival journey of my father and grandfather Samuel. We wanted to find Little Kalno Street and intended to do so on foot, like we had done on our previous visits to Riga.

We left our hotel in Kr. Valdemara Street and walked toward Brivibas Street until we reached the big building, where it all began. It was cold outside; the sky was gray and the wind that blew in from the river only made it colder. We stood for just a moment in front of the towering gray building, wrapped in coats, scarves, gloves and beanie hats, looked at the building and then continued on our way. Before we had set out, we looked at the city Streets Map of Riga and found out that Little Kalno Street was on the other side of the city. We realized that we had a long way ahead of us, despite the bitter cold.

As we moved away from the city business center we felt and saw a growing neglect: older homes with their paint peeling that had seen better days, broken sidewalks and weeds growing in every corner. So too, our sense of personal security was dropping. The further we went, the fewer people we met. Eventually we saw a Pravoslav church a short distance ahead, painted white with three turrets with a kind of onion-shaped crown at the top of each, painted dark gray. We assumed that we'd arrived at the right place. We searched the area trying to find Little Kalno Street, but no street we saw bore that name. We got closer to the church and only when we were right in front of it did we see the entrance to Little Kalno Street: a narrow street, which gradually sloped downward while curving to the right. From where we stood, we couldn't see the other end. Old single-story and two-story wooden houses stood on both sides of the street between concrete buildings of a few levels. All the houses were very old and very neglected.

We had no doubt that most of the wooden houses in the

street were already there, back then in September 1941, when Grandpa Samuel moved his family to live in this street, that was part of the ghetto. One could assume that almost seventy years before Grandpa Samuel had stood in the same place we were standing, seeing more or less the same street scenery we were looking at. But what a difference. While we stood there as tourists, Grandpa Samuel had come to the same place, hunted, and feeling the noose tightening around his and his family's necks.

We began walking down the street. We had no idea which one of the houses hosted the Gutkin extended family within its walls. Assa took out a camera and began taking pictures of the old houses: a two-story wooden house painted brown with three windows on its ground floor and white curtains hiding the interior of the house; an old three-story house made of stone with a style that showed it had been built many years ago; a two-story green wooden house with a red sloping roof and a white frame around each of the four windows that faced the front street. Thus, house by house.

We reached the bend in the street and could finally see the end of it. The street was indeed short and one could see that it ended in a large square where there were a number of transit stations.

We continued on our way until we found ourselves standing in front of a small wooden house, empty and deserted. Painted a turquoise green with large openings in the front wall, which meant that once there were two large windows, and two other openings, one of which was probably the entrance. The roof was made of metal slabs, brown from rust with two cuckoo clock vents rising above, which resembled a dark maw. The house stood lonely and radiated an atmosphere of disrepair and neglect of many years. On one side of the house there was a little garden that separated it from a neighboring wooden house and on the other side, a vacant lot that was used as a garbage disposal for the residents of the street.

It was the first house that resembled the description I'd heard from my father about where he and his family had taken refuge sixty-eight years before. Was it *the* house? My father hadn't described the cuckoo roof vents, but maybe he just hadn't remembered that detail. I looked at the deserted house and tried to feel it, get some kind of a message, a hint that it remembered the occupants from years past. But the house remained silent, refusing to disclose its secrets and leaving us with the freedom to imagine the past as we pleased.

We took a picture of the house and moved on. Within a few minutes we reached the large square at the end of the street, where we saw more neglect and disrepair, and a number of residents that seemed to be drunk. The atmosphere was very unpleasant. After a short wait in the bitter cold, we boarded a tram that returned us to the city center.

***

Aunt Ljuba and Uncle Naum also had to move to the ghetto. They had lived in Palestine since 1934, as Jews free from any anti-Semitism, but their decision in 1938 to extend their stay in Latvia caused them to find themselves in the Riga ghetto along with the rest of the Riga Jews, and eventually sealed their fate. Their children were of course in Palestine and at the time had no idea about what was happening to them.

The next few days we saw the Germans surround the ghetto with barbed wire and build entrance and exit gates. While watching the work carried out by the Germans I felt, reluctantly, that they didn't have any technical skills and if they would only let me give them instructions, the job would be done much more efficiently. As absurd as sounds, my technical talents bugged me in that context, as if it was a professional matter and not one affecting my life and the life of my family.

Grandpa Samuel tells us:

They put approximately 30,000 residents in the ghetto. A Judenrat appointed by the German occupation authorities dealt with the management of all the issues of the Jewish population in the ghetto. The chairman of the Judenrat was a Jewish lawyer whose name was Rosenthal. His replacement was former Latvian ex-under officer from Jewish descent called Engineer Vazbuzky. The headquarters of the SS, which was in charge of all the various matters related to Jews in the ghetto, was in the ghetto. The commander of the ghetto was an SS-Fuhrer named Krause. He was about forty, medium height, blond, with a solid build and a round face. One of the officers who helped him was an SS Unter-Fuhrer named Tuchler. He was between 25 to 30 year's old, medium height and thin.

On Saturday, October 25th 1941, we saw that the Germans had completed the construction of the fence. They closed the entrance and exit gates and locked them with a chain. Two German soldiers were stationed outside the main gate. The ghetto was closed: no way in and no way out. Inside our crowded apartment nobody said a word. They didn't have to. It was clear to all of us that this was going to be bad, but we didn't know, or didn't want to guess, what was waiting for us. That night I had trouble getting to sleep. I kept asking myself what would happen tomorrow.

The next day we were told that the Germans had ordered all the men and boys to report to work at five o'clock the next morning at the main gate. It was another night without sleep. The next morning we turned up, my father, Ze'eva and me, along with all the other men in the ghetto, near the main gate at five o'clock in the morning. There were masses of men. At least I was with the men. I felt that if I had been left with my mother, Robby and Aunt Fanny, I would have felt a lot worse.

The Judenrat members divided us into groups. They did this by shouting and it took a long time, but before long they were able to sort some ten thousand people into work groups. My father, Ze'eva and I were told to join a group of four other men and stand together. The rest of my relatives who lived with us in the ghetto got assigned to other work groups. Volya Gutkin was disabled and was therefore exempt from work.

A few minutes later we started walking, escorted by two Latvians and one German soldier, the three of them armed with rifles. We had no idea where they were taking us to, but the direction was along the Daugava River in a southeasterly direction. At first we passed a neglected area of Riga city, where we ran into a group of Latvians who approached us and swore at us, as if we did them some harm. But I knew that it wasn't why they hated us. It's because we were Jews. After what I'd been through in the last month, it only added to my general sense of powerlessness and my general uncertainty about the future. But with the same breath, I felt that If only I could, I would pounce on them and 'break their bones'. After all, I wasn't afraid of them. I was strong and I knew that on a 'one on one' battle I could overcome each and every one of them, and only because of my "situation", I couldn't do it at the time.

We continued walking in a crowded group, periodically bumping into each other, and almost falling. I walked behind my father and Ze'eva, who was walking beside him. Lately I preferred not to look at my father's face. My father, the strong and powerful man, no longer seemed that way. His eyes were very tired and showed endless worry. Everything we had been through I could handle, but accepting the fact that my father wasn't all mighty as before was above my powers. I preferred to walk behind him.

This march lasted about three hours. For some men this walk was beyond their powers and they were slowing down, panting and gasping, only a shout from one of the armed escorts driving them to find the strength to keep up with the other men. At the end of this long walk we arrived at a place called Salaspils, which was an agricultural area. We were led to a field that belonged to a local farmer that had potatoes scattered all over. We were told to collect the potatoes into fifty-kilogram sacks and close them. I remembered working on the farmer's farm two years before but this time everything looked completely different.

After a few hours of work, my back and my knees started to hurt. Later on, my fingers ached so much that I couldn't even catch the potatoes with my hands. The work became a nightmare for me. I guess that the older peoples' situation was much worse. From time to time, I looked at my father and Ze'eva who worked next to me; they were very tired from the effort. At 3 o'clock in the afternoon the Latvian field owner brought a pot of soup and a large lump of bread. The armed escorts told us that this was lunch for us and we were given a half-hour lunch break. The adults got organized and distributed the food among us in an orderly fashion. At the end of the break, we continued to work until five o'clock in the afternoon. It began to darken and the temperature started falling, so I was very glad when the armed escorts told us that our working day had ended. They told us to get organized as we were on our way to Salaspils, and we started walking back to the ghetto.

Walking back was exhausting and it felt like every step I made drained what energy I still had left in me. Naturally, no one talked the whole way. Only at eight o'clock in the evening did we reach the ghetto, in complete darkness. When we got to the main gate, we stood in a long line and a soldier searched every one of us. Everyone's pockets were emptied in front of everyone, and whatever we had hidden in those pockets, any food we'd brought back so that our families in the ghetto would have something to eat, was taken out. We were warned that anyone who was caught with food on his return to the ghetto would be shot on the spot. This was the first time that the realization that these people were going to kill us really penetrated my bones, and it was very scary. I looked at my father and saw that his eyes were dull, his head was down and he was more exhausted than me. Only Ze'eva seemed somehow recovered to some extent and it was enough to encourage me to go on.

The next morning we showed up again at five o'clock in the morning at the main gate to what seemed like a repeat of yesterday. At least this time I knew what was expected, and that helped me get through the day. My father seemed as if he had recovered. At the end of the second day, when we returned exhausted to the ghetto, my father sat with my mother and Ze'eva on the doorstep of the entrance to the wooden house and said in a loud and clear voice that we needed to find a way to "fit" in an easier job, otherwise we wouldn't survive for long.

We continued working in a team sent to Salaspils for a few more days and one could almost say that we had become accustomed to it. But one morning, ten days later, we were lucky when my father, Ze'eva and I got assigned to a team of 12 men, which included an attorney named Levinson, one man called Dickman, whom we later realized that like my father, used to work with wood, and one named Tislovich Fritz whom we knew from before, as he had also lived in an apartment in the big building. Tislovich was older than me by 15 years, but he was a very nice man who used to join me and his nieces when we played together. They were my age and also lived in the big building. There were others, but I can't remember their names.

Our team was sent to carry out work in a public building in no. 30 Ģertrūdes Street in Riga, only a twenty-minute walk from the ghetto. It was of course a dramatic change compared to the previous ten working days. A German soldier with a rifle accompanied us to the building.

It was a brown, five-story building adjacent to other similar tall buildings. It had large windows in front with a big opening leading to an inner courtyard. It was similar to the courtyard in our big building. The courtyard was not paved and had an entrance to the basement at the end.

The public building we were sent to was used as a residential house for German girls who worked as clerks at the post office, and were all wearing a jacket on which a symbol of lightning was embedded. As soon as we arrived, a high-ranking German officer in an SS Communications German Corps uniform (Nachrichten) accepted us, and to clarify his important position in this building and his extensive powers, he told us that he was the building manager.

He explained to us what our duties were: to clean the inside of the whole building every day, including windows, rooms and stairways, to take care of operating the two furnaces in the building, one for heating the building and the other for the hot water and to dry the firewood that arrived damp and moist. At five o'clock in the afternoon we had to light the stoves in each one of the girls' bedrooms and prepare a pile of dry firewood logs large enough to keep it running for the whole night. He did not humiliate us, so my first impression was that he was not an immediate enemy. On the other hand, he didn't show any empathy towards us, either.

Due to the fact that Latvia is situated in Northern Europe, it's already very cold in October. Therefore, residential heating is a basic and significant requirement in everyday life. The heating was done using stoves heated by firewood logs.

In order to provide firewood logs to heat the German girls' bedrooms, a kind of a small plant was built in the basement. Every few days, shipments of fresh logs arrived by truck, green and moist. We had to dry the wood, chop it and prepare it in the form of ready-made sized firewood logs to be used in the stoves. After that we had to bring the logs out of the basement and arrange a pile of ready-to-use firewood logs next to each stove in each bedroom. When my father heard what our task was he was really happy; his body straightened and it seemed like new blood was pumping through his body. My father loved working with wood and its smell in the air; he really 'understood' wood because of his many years of experience as the owner of the Zunde wood plant. Working with wood was a source of comfort for me as well, since it reminded me of better days.

From our first day of work in that building, it was clear to the building manager that he had both an effective and very grateful team being employed in the building. Thus, when the German troops arrived to escort us back to the ghetto, he asked them to make sure that from now on, this team, with the same people would be sent to him every day. And so it was. Each passing day the team had become more efficient and the building manager didn't hide his satisfaction from us, although he didn't do anything practical to reward us.

The German girls ignored us completely, as if we were part of the building's walls, but they didn't bother us. They noticed that their rooms were properly heated and that we took care of their needs. From time to time, we would find some food that had been deliberately left for us on the plates in their dining room, and I began to notice which of the girls had left food for us and which girls hadn't.

My father was fully recovered and soon began to manage all basement activities. He also started to get his talent for business back. One evening after returning to the ghetto, and after I told him about what I discovered about the girls who had left us food, he gathered me and Ze'eva and told us, "From now on, you put dry wood logs beside the stove in the rooms of the German girls who leave food for us, and those who don't leave us any food will get wet wood logs that I'll get for you from the basement, until they start leaving us proper food." And so it was. A girl that didn't leave us any food discovered very quickly that the wood logs she had received were damp and didn't burn well, and she was cold at night. Most of the girls took the hint and left us food in the dining room. Following this, we had plenty to eat and we were never hungry.

We would smuggle some of the food in the evening to the ghetto for our families. There wasn't a lot of food in the ghetto. Ghetto residents were allowed a meager official ration of 100 grams of bread and 30 grams of meat per day. But it wasn't 'hunger' yet.

We often stayed to sleep in the warm basement following

the building manager's instructions and only one of us went back to the ghetto. So those of us who returned to the ghetto took food with them. It was still a big risk because of the inspections at the gates, so when we knew that a search for food was held at the main gate, we would throw away the food before arriving at the gate, without our escorts noticing (or noticing but ignoring).

Two months went by during which we strengthened and recovered from the blows we'd suffered since the beginning of the German occupation, both physically and mentally. My father came to himself and radiated a lot of confidence, from which I drew confidence, too.

As usual, my relationship with Ze'eva was as it had been before the War, no special 'chemistry'. He saw me as his little brother who didn't really need attention and I saw in him my elder brother, who may have been very knowledgeable, a true scholar, but lacked any technical skills and was not a working man.

In the ghetto, there was also a sense that the situation was stabilizing and different kinds of activities had begun. Among others, a sort of indirect trading between ghetto residents and local Latvian merchants was going on. The Latvian merchants risked a severe punishment from the Germans if they were caught, yet decided to trade with the inhabitants of the ghetto, because of the nice profits they made. As the Germans confiscated all funds held by the Jews and forbade Jews to hold money, an alternative mechanism of payment had developed. It turned out that prior to moving to the ghetto, many Jews had deposited money with their Latvian friends. Those Latvians became a kind of private bank and they paid the merchants for the goods that they supplied.

I know that many times the Latvians kept the money deposited in their hands for themselves, but it turned out that there were quite a few honest Latvians who 'kept their word'. In addition, some of the Jews hid gold coins on their bodies when they entered the ghetto and that way they had the means to buy different goods they needed.

CHAPTER FOUR

DEATH AND RESCUE
1941-1943

November-December 1941
November 27, 1941

On November 27th 1941, the ghetto command in Riga posted notices announcing extensive procedures. The posters stated that men between the ages of 18 and 60 who were able to work had to report at the ghetto gate on Firsa Sadovnikova St. on 29 November, in order to move into the new partial ghetto. All of the other ghetto inhabitants would have to leave for an outside camp that had been designated their new place of residence. There they would be drawn on for lighter forms of labor. Each person was permitted to take 20kg (44lbs) of personal belongings as hand baggage. In addition, it could be inferred from the poster that the ghetto would be cleared street by street[5].

The next day, an electric fence was built around a small

---

5   The Final Solution in Riga: Exploitation and Annihilation, 1941-1944, pp. 136-137.

part of the ghetto and separated it from the rest of the ghetto. The Germans' intention was to transfer all the working men to the part that was separated from the rest of the ghetto, nicknamed the "small ghetto", and start killing all the other residents of the ghetto.

But on the morning of November 29th 1941, while the men stood waiting for instructions, the employers of the different groups of Jews, including representatives of the German army who also employed hundreds of Jews in different construction works in Riga, arrived. It turned out that the ghetto command hadn't updated the German army and the various employers regarding their plans. The commanders of the ghetto and the 'employers' started to argue. They needed the labor force of their Jews and feared that it would harm the program to start the extermination of the Jews of Riga. Eventually, the officers of the ghetto allowed the different employers to take only 'their' permanent employees. All the other Jews who were not identified specifically as permanent employees of work groups whose employees had arrived to take them, were refused admittance to the "small ghetto" and remained in the ghetto[6].

***

The Germans set up the "small ghetto". It was clear that something was going to happen. In light of the order of the camp command the day before, our work team returned to

---

6   The Final Solution in Riga: Exploitation and Annihilation, 1941-1944, pp. 138.

the ghetto at the end of the day's work, November 28th 1941. On Saturday, November 29, we stood as stipulated in the camp command's order, fearing what was going to come.

Grandpa Samuel tells us:

At the end of November 1941 the Jewish Order Service ordered[7] that all adult Jewish men were to be called up. The order stated that we could take a hand baggage weighing 20kg. When we stood on the street, Vazbuzky, who was Acting Commander of the OD, passed me and said to me in Russian, "This is the beginning of the end." We stood on the street for several hours and noticed the German managers of the work places where we were employed, who demanded their employees back. At some stage, Vazbuzky went to the ghetto headquarters offices. When he returned, he looked a little calmer and he told me, "I think the sun is starting to shine a little bit". Soon after, we were taken back to our workplaces.

After a while we got an order to go to work as usual. We went towards the public building, walking in a group with an armed escort, like the past three weeks. It wasn't snowing, but it was very cold and even walking from the ghetto couldn't keep us warm because of our poor clothes.

I couldn't wait to get to the building and go down to the

7　　The OD, the Jewish Order Service.

warm basement. During the day nothing unusual happened that could explain what happened that evening. At six o'clock in the evening, shortly before we had to get ready to return to the ghetto, the German building manager came, his face all grim, and while shouting he demanded that the whole group report to him immediately at the entrance to the building. My father sent me to get Ze'eva who was still busy with the distribution of the wood logs in the top floor bedrooms, and I went up running to get him. Ze'eva argued that he hadn't finished putting the wood logs in all the rooms, but I insisted he leave everything and come down with me as fast as possible. Ze'eva joined me with a curious face and we went down the stairs together to the entrance of the building.

When we got there, all the other members of the group were concentrated, looking concerned in front of the manager of the building, who looked very angry and waved his arms in all directions.

Without any prior warning, the building manager began yelling at all of us in German that we hadn't done our job properly the past few days, the building was very dirty inside and out and that we needed to clean the whole building immediately, all its parts and all its floors. "I am very angry with you", he shouted, "You suck. You are bums. You do not deserve to go back to the ghetto tonight, so you will clean the building during the night and when you finish, you will stay to sleep in the basement, and tomorrow ... we shall see."

I had no idea what he was talking about. The building looked perfectly clean, certainly cleaner than it was on the first day we arrived as a work group to the building. He started rushing us to take our cleaning equipment at once and except for one of us who has to stay on duty in the basement, all the rest were required to clean the entire building. We worked all night without a break and only towards the morning did we go back to the basement, exhausted, and tried to catch some sleep on the floor. In the morning, after the German girls left their bedrooms, we cleaned their rooms too.

The next day, in the morning, the building manager came. He checked our work thoroughly and again started to yell again at us that we had not done our work thoroughly and demanded again that we re-clean the building. I had no idea what he wanted from us, the building looked completely clean. When I asked my father what he thought about it, he shrugged his shoulders and said, "If this is what this 'Goy'[8] wants, let it be, just continue cleaning" and ended the matter.

Thus, for ten days, the building manager wouldn't let us return to the ghetto, using various excuses. None of us tried to understand him or his reasons any longer. Only on the evening of December 9th 1941, when the building manager eventually let us return to the ghetto at the end of the day's work, did we realize that his goal had been to save our lives. The reality we saw in the ghetto was horrid and hit us mercilessly.

As we got closer to the ghetto, we could feel the change. It took us but a moment to realize that there were hardly any people; it was empty. The ghetto was closed and instead, there was a much smaller ghetto, which included 'little Kalno' as well. We waited impatiently to cross the gate and we rushed

---

8   A gentile

to the two-story house where we'd left my mother and Robby, Aunt Fanny and her two sons, Uncle Boris's widow, Aunt Nina and her two daughters, Gena and Rachel, ten days ago. The house was empty. There was no one there. We tried to find out if they could be found elsewhere in the ghetto, but in vain. They hadn't left any trace. Aunt Ljuba and Uncle Naum had disappeared too, like they had never existed. My father collapsed on the threshold of the door, started mumbling words in Yiddish and was stuck there for hours. It seemed like he just refused to enter the house. Ze'eva sat in another corner of the empty house and too refused to talk. There were terrible rumors: one said that they'd killed them all out of town, but we had trouble believing that. It was incomprehensible. A different rumor said that they had all been taken to another camp outside the city.

We found out later that on November 29th 1941, i.e. at the end of the first day we had been 'punished' by the building manager, the Germans and their Latvian collaborators began performing the first 'Action' in the ghetto. The ghetto residents who had reported early in the morning that same day in the square in front of the main gate, and the men who were not taken by their 'employers', were joined by a group of about a thousand Jews that arrived in a rail transport, probably from Germany, just the day before. They were divided into groups and were ordered to march several kilometers towards the Rumbula forest east of Riga, not far from the Rumbula Train Station. There, they were sent in groups of five people to stand on the edge of the pre-prepared pits and were shot in the following method: 5 Jews standing with their faces towards the edge of the pit and 10 shooters behind them. They assigned two shooters per Jew. The first shooter aimed at the head and the second one aimed at the back. Mothers were ordered to hold their little ones close to the chest so that the bullet aimed at the back would kill the child, too. After the gunshots, the shooters checked if anyone was still alive. Anyone who had survived was shot again, this time in the head. The pits had become mass graves.

About six thousand Jews who were left for some reason and slipped the first 'Action', were concentrated in the small ghetto. In the rest of the vacated ghetto, "the large ghetto", a group of about a thousand Jews, who had arrived in rail transports from Western Europe only one day after the first 'Action', was housed.

On December 8th 1941, the day before our return to the ghetto, the second and last 'Action' that wiped the remaining Jews left in the ghetto, both the old ghetto residents and the other Jews who came to the ghetto after the first 'Action', was performed.

Only a few survived the first 'Action' and the second 'Action' and lived to tell us what had happened. They are those who told us that all our family members, including my mother and little Robby, were among the Ghetto residents taken in the first 'Action'.

We didn't have any hope or illusion that my mother and Robby might have been saved. We had a cold and bitter understanding that that was it; they were gone. No last-minute embrace, not a chance to say words of good-bye. They were gone forever.

Grandpa Samuel tells us:

I met an ex-employee of mine named Zaolis who was dressed in an SS uniform. He told me that all the Jews were shot in a forest, which was located about 13 kilometers outside the city, in the region of Salaspils. He also told me that he himself participated in the executions.

I asked him how it was possible that a decent person who worked with me for 15 years could take part in such a thing. To that he replied that before the Actions started, the German gave the Latvians so much schnapps to drink, that they no longer knew what they were doing.

It was generally known that the ghetto commander, SS Fuhrer Krause, led the extermination Actions. A special unit of the SS carried out the Actions and the Latvians were stationed during the Actions mainly as guards. I met a woman who was not injured, but fell into the mass grave during the extermination and had managed to climb out of the ditch afterwards, and with the help of a Latvian peasant woman was able to return to Riga to the small ghetto. I don't remember the woman's name. She told me that the victims were gathered in the forest in places where mass graves had already been dug. The victims were led in groups to the areas of those ditches and ordered to undress. The victims had to fold their clothes themselves. After which they were taken to the ditches and shot using machine guns. The shots were made by German and Latvian groups of the SS. The victims were forced to descend into the ditches that were excavated in the form of stairs, lie at the bottom and then they were shot.

The next morning, we returned to work in the building in no. 30 Ģertrūdes Street. We continued working there for another year and a half, one day after another, until June 1943. Having been the youngest in the working group, I had no real connection with anyone else, except of course Ze'eva and my father. The only exception was Fritz Tislovich; my father had asked him to teach me different subjects in place of the years of study I had lost, and he spoke to me many times during that period.

December 2009, Israel

I have been meeting with my father every Saturday morning for a Story Hour Since July 2009. My father and I would sit on the terrace in the garden, I would ask, and he would answer. Telling the Story about finding the ghetto empty without his family exhausted him. He was not prepared to continue talking about his experiences during the War.

Three months had gone by and he was still firm. I continued asking and he continued refusing: "You exhaust me", he told me. "But you promised", I replied". "So I promised..." he told me and turned away. I got up and stood behind him and asked, "So what did you do for a year and a half in the building in Ģertrūdes Street?" And before my father could reply I continued with another question: "What did you talk about the next day? What did you do for a year and a half?" He looked at me angrily and continued walking slowly away from me without giving me a single glance.

Finally, my father relented and agreed to continue his story.

***

The large ghetto didn't stay empty for long. The Germans began populating it with the thousands of Jews who were transported from all over Western Europe (primarily from Germany, the Netherlands and France), en route to their final extermination, in the forests around Riga.

Between them and us there was a barbed wire fence to prevent the passage from the small ghetto to the large ghetto, but it was possible to speak to them through the fence. I managed to speak in German to some German Jews a number of times. They were very miserable, disconnected completely from their birthplace, in a strange place where the language was either Russian or Latvian. While we could use some help from the local Latvian population from time to time, they didn't have any means to communicate with them.

But their suffering didn't last long, because shortly after being brought to the large ghetto they would be taken somewhere else and never returned. Even in this context there were many different rumors, which all had one thing in common - the end of those Jews was very bad and tragic.

Grandpa Samuel tells us:

In January 1942, transports of Jews from Germany arrived in the large ghetto in Riga. A Jew, who lived with me in the small ghetto and whose name I cannot remember, had told me that he had been working at the Riga Train Station when a transport of very well-dressed German Jews arrived. They came as train passengers, with their baggage, without any guarded escorts. Krause, who had waited for them at the train station, gave them a speech and explained that they had arrived to work, but that they needed to get washed first. They were put on buses and I found out later that they were taken to the forest where they were shot immediately. Only a fraction of the Jews transported to Riga, those with good physical fitness, eventually came to the ghetto. Those Jews remained in Riga and were put to work. As far as I can recall, transport from Hanover, Berlin, Prague and other cities in Germany and Czechoslovakia came to Riga.

At that time it was published in the ghetto that the elderly, the sick and the weak were taken to work in what was known as "the production of canned Dunaminder". Trucks often came with SS men who took those people to the Dunaminder Canning Factory. Much later, we found out from Latvian soldiers guarding us, that there never had been a canning factory named Dunaminder. The people had been taken from the ghetto and shot in the woods.

We returned to the building at 30 Ģertrūdes Street. We were a group of 12 people with no family. We had nothing left except for our bodies and the clothes we were wearing. It was clear to us that we had nothing to look for in the ghetto. The adults decided to try and convince the building manager to agree to let us live in the basement of the building and not return to the ghetto any more. It was agreed that my father, as the leader of the group, would bring this issue up with the building manager.

One day, my father approached the building manager respectfully and asked him to let us stay in the basement of the building instead of returning each evening to the ghetto. He justified this by the intense cold and the need to maintain the ovens in the rooms, all day and all night, and feed them all the time with more and more firewood. He explained that the logs that get to the building were damp and poor quality. The building manager knew on the one hand that the Jews had to return to the ghetto every night, but on the other hand, the reason my father had given him made sense to him. Although he was a declared Nazi, the building manager understood that father's offer held a common interest shared by him and his Jewish staff. He thought it over, and reached a decision: "I have no objection, but remember that you should not leave the building at all. Anyone caught outside risks instant death, and you should know that you won't get anything here, not even food. How you get along, that's your problem." And he left. It was enough for us to ensure that we wouldn't have to return to the ghetto every day and that we would continue to stay in a place that was heated in the coming cold winter.

We stayed on living in the basement of the building, all of us together. We ate leftovers that the girls had left us in the dining room or that we found in the kitchen, which we shared. But we were still hungry every day as the food was not enough to make us feel full. We had to get another source of food, and also get some clothes, shoes and other items that a group of men needed in order to maintain a basic lifestyle in the basement of a building.

One of the adults in the team said that a number of Latvians still owed him a lot of money from before the transfer to the ghetto, and that they were a kind of personal bank to be used for him and could help buy food on the 'outside'. He offered to leave the building at night, secretly, to contact them and ask them to buy food as part of their debt. When asked if he was not afraid that they would turn him in to the Germans, the meaning of which was clear and known, he said that he trusted them not to turn on him, and in any case we didn't have a choice. And so it was, he left for the city and returned in the morning with food for all of us. After this successful experience, other adults decided to risk themselves, get out to town at night, and contact Latvian friends requesting them to sell us some food, using similar 'personal banks'.

Consequently, once every two or three weeks one of the adults would secretly go to town, to Latvian friends who were willing to help, to catch up on the news and buy food. Living in the building had become a sad daily routine with the sole purpose of surviving one day after another. This is how we survived in the building for a year and a half.

Winter 1941-1942

Winter 1941-1942 was particularly cold, even compared to what I had known in previous winters. We worked very hard all winter to heat the rooms in the building. The basement was also cold. When spring came, we were glad that we had managed to survive that winter. I knew it wasn't obvious. The news that reached us from time to time was depressing: the Germans advanced and besieged Moscow and Leningrad, strengthening their control over the entire region. It was a bad sign for us. Deep down in my heart I knew that our arrangement here in this building wouldn't last indefinitely. I was afraid of the future, but I tried to suppress it and I didn't say a word to father or Ze'eva, but I assumed that they too had similar thoughts going through their heads.

CHAPTER FIVE

RUMBULA FOREST

October 1993, Rumbula Forest

Only two years had passed since Latvia was freed from the Soviet Empire embrace and signs of the previous regime could still be seen everywhere. The poor maintenance of the public roads and houses, sparse cars on the roads, the extreme caution that Latvians would take when approaching strangers, and much more. There were only very few hotels and the prices of the rooms were very expensive. It was difficult to find a decent hotel at a reasonable price in those days. Moreover, one had to fill out different forms whenever you left the hotel and the general feeling one got was that of being followed all the time.

My father came to Riga two weeks before me and by the time I had arrived, he had already booked two rooms for us in the apartment of a local Jewish woman who flew to Germany on vacation. The apartment was comfortable, but it was very cold. The central heating system of the apartment didn't work and there was no other means of heating, except for blankets. It was very cold outside as well, even though it was only

October, and winter wasn't expected for another month and a half. When my father checked why the central heating wasn't working in the apartment, he found out that it was the situation all over Riga. There was a dispute between Latvia and Russia, who at the time was Latvia's supplier of oil, and in response, the Russians had greatly reduced the amount of oil transferred to Latvia. Consequently, Riga's municipality decided to save energy and refrained from using the central heating system. The result being that I was very cold, both outside and inside the apartment. In order to take a shower, we had to heat water in a large pot on the stove in the apartment and pour the hot water into the small bath we had in the apartment, to which we added cold water, which of course was abundant.

Fifty years after leaving it secretly, my father came to Riga to find out what happened to the vast amount of property that his family had had on the eve of the War. By the time I had arrived, he had already searched the places he remembered and had also hired the services of a local lawyer, Mrs. Ita Starobina, a classmate who had studied with him in Hebrew School and had started taking care of locating the documents and following the various legal proceedings. Within a short while, it became clear that locating the property and returning it to its original owner would be a long process. But it was the first step, because as we all know, "a journey of a thousand miles begins with a single step" (ancient Chinese proverb).

The day after my arrival, my father took me on a tour of the city. Our first stop was the big building where he grew up. The building was neglected and it was clear that it had known much better days. He couldn't take me inside apartment no.

11 at the first entrance, because he didn't know the people who were living there; they were strangers to him and he chose not to bother them at this stage. At least that was what he told me.

We then started walking slowly along Miera Street. Before long, I smelled the sweet smell of chocolate in the air. When I told my father that I thought I could smell chocolate, he laughed and told me that it was the next surprise waiting for me. Within a few minutes we got to a gray building with large, thick wooden doors with a sign written in the Latin alphabet: LAIMA. My father opened one of the doors and went inside and I followed him.

I found myself in front of a shop full of sweets. Now I understood that we'd arrived at the source of the 'tasty' smell. As we were standing in the entrance plaza in front of the store, my father told me that the plant had been purchased and developed during the mid-twentieth century by friends of Grandfather Samuel (Mr. Frumchenko, Mr. Kopilov, Mr. Segal and Mr. Moshevitz) who immigrated to Palestine in the 1930's and built the ELITE factory in Ramat Gan.

We entered the store and it was the first time I'd used Latvian money. I bought all the candy I could set my hands on, including chocolate rabbits coated with foil, which I later brought as gifts for my children upon my return to Israel. Only then did we realize that the chocolate rabbits weren't hollow like in the West, but completely filled with delicious chocolate. For the rest of the day we walked through different places in Riga which were milestones from my father's childhood.

The next day, my father told me he wanted to take me to a special place. What the place was and why it was special, he would not say, but he promised to explain when we got there. We took a taxi and my father told the driver in Russian where he wanted him to take us. The look that the taxi driver had on his face gave a hint that there was something very unusual at that destination, but in those days, for money, a taxi driver would take us anywhere.

The taxi drove along Brivibas Street and turned onto a main road that passed through rows and rows of gray and unsightly housing developments that all looked identical. At some point I noticed that we'd left town. The scenery was full of autumn trees with lots of brown, yellowish fallen leaves at their feet. I remembered the picture of a European autumn we'd learned about in school: a gray sky with trees in the background. I liked this view better than the housing projects we had passed. As this was my first visit to Latvia and specifically to Riga, everything I saw was new to me.

We then drove east along the Daugava River that the city of Riga is built next to, with the taxi driver maneuvering between numerous holes in the road that clearly hadn't had proper maintenance for many years and was in various stages of disintegration. To my right, the Daugava River was flowing, its waters dark and gloomy. And to my left, I saw a combination of industrial buildings with rusty brown cranes which were surrounded by gray concrete walls with high green weeds growing at their sides. The landscape quickly changed to an endless forest of trees, impossible to see the end of.

The taxi turned left and went up on a dirt road that crossed the forest. That road was even bumpier than the asphalt road that we'd previously taken. The drive on the dirt road was short and ended in a small square in the heart of the forest. My father turned to the Russian taxi driver and asked him to wait for us for half an hour. I obviously didn't understand what was going on and was very curious about why my father had brought me here. Two things caught my eye immediately: the first was that the area of the forest north of the parking spot was significantly higher than the rest of the forest area around us, and that the trees were much younger than the rest of the forest. The second was that at a distance of about five meters from where we stood, there was a metal plaque with an inscription in Russian which I didn't understand, as well as a number of dates, one of which I recognized from a distance: 30.11.1941.

"What is written on this plaque?" I asked my father.

"Have you heard of a place called Rumbula? This is Rumbula", my father answered with a question and answered it, too.

Because the name meant nothing to me, I asked what it was.

"This is the place where our family was murdered during the Holocaust, as well as all the Jews in Riga and many Jews that were brought here from other places in Europe to be exterminated" my father replied.

"But what does the plaque say?" I asked again.

My father didn't translate the plaque, but explained to me that it said that in this place the Germans murdered Soviet citizens, without specifying that they were Jews.

He started walking on a dirt trail leading up the hill into the woods. I joined him. At the end of the trail we reached a kind of clearing, covered with weeds but without any trees. At the side of the clearing, one could see the margins of a big rectangle that looked as if they were marked on the ground. These rectangles could be seen in every direction we looked.

"Those are the pits where they threw the bodies of the Jews that they shot here", my father said. The clearing was completely surrounded by those pits.

Except for that, there was nothing that hinted at the horrors that had happened here fifty-two years before. Not a sign, not any other marks.

"I wonder what those trees would tell us if they could only talk", I told my father, and he replied that these trees were planted after the War, to cover the pits. Now I understood why these trees seemed younger than the other trees of the forest.

We were there for half an hour but despite all my efforts, I couldn't imagine what had happened there. Perhaps because it was simply inconceivable. We walked back on the narrow trail through the forest and returned to town in the taxi.

June 2004
Rumbula Forest

11 years passed since I visited the massacre site in Rumbula Forest, and I had the opportunity to visit the place again. This time the site of the massacre was properly maintained. A paved and winding path rose from the parking area and the entrance gate between the tall, green forest trees rising up to infinity. Bright green, leafy shrubs filled the space between the trees. Everything was so quiet and so peaceful.

Every curve offered a new perspective to the forest and its sounds. I enjoyed the walk in the woods and how relaxed it made me feel. The path ended in a large gravel courtyard. The transition was sharp and difficult to digest: the edges of the killing pits that were still visible that day marked the sides of the courtyard, reminding every visitor that they hadn't come here looking for peace and tranquility, but for the memory of the horror that had occurred right here.

In the middle of a wide square, rising to the height of about three meters, stood a dark stone statue of the seven-branched candelabrum ('Menora'), the stationing of which had been initiated by the Jewish community of Riga. At the foot of the statue and surrounding it in small triangular shaped compounds, together forming a Star of David, were small tombstones in local granite colors - gray, brown and reddish. Every stone bore multiple family names; one could easily identify that they were all were Jewish.

I checked what it was and I was told that the community allowed the family members of those killed in the Holocaust to have a memorial stone, for a fee, of course. The decision was immediately made. I had the opportunity to set a tombstone for the Gutkin family, including all its various branches, and all that remained was to get the full list of names from my father.

When I returned to Israel, I asked my father for the list of names of all our family members who had died in the Holocaust in Riga. "Why do you need these names?" asked my father. Initially he refused, then relented and gave me the list, and asked me not to involve him with any matters concerning this issue anymore.

I turned to Mr. Zenia Falkenstein, one of my father's local friends, a few years younger than him. I told him that I wanted to put three memory tombstones engraved with the names of my family members. I also asked him if he would be willing to handle the preparation of the tombstones and deal with the members of the Jewish community on my behalf. Zenia said that he would gladly do it for me.

The massacre site in Rumbula forest, 1993

The massacre site in Rumbula forest, 2004

Mr. Zenia Falkenstein at the entrance to the massacre site
in Rumbula forest, 2004

CHAPTER SIX

LENTA CAMP
1943 - 1944

Towards the end of 1942, the Germans decided to eliminate all remnants of the ghettos in Latvia, stop employing the Jews working in the small work groups scattered in different places, and relocate all remaining Jews to one concentration camp.

For this purpose, they established a concentration camp in March 1943 (at the end of winter, and the beginning of the thawing of the frozen ground) on the outskirts of Riga, not far from the luxurious neighborhood of Mežaparks. It was called the Kaiserwald Concentration Camp. Prisoners of war from various nationalities who had been transferred to Latvia had built the camp. A crematorium had also been built and was operated in the camp.

Coinciding with the establishment of the building of the Kaiserwald Camp, multiple sub-camps were built in the Riga neighborhood: Strazdenhof Camp, Lenta Camp (Lenta - SD Werkstaette Lenta Security Service Repair Shop) on the other side of the Daugava River, the VEF Factory and the leather factory in Ūdens Street in Riga.

After the completion of the Kaiserwald Camp, the Germans began transferring the rest of the Jews that were left in Latvia. A few of them were Latvian Jews, but most of them were Jews who continued to be transported from Western Europe.

At the same time, the Germans were busy destroying the ghettos in Latvia and sending some of the Jews from the Riga ghetto directly to Auschwitz, a distance of a few hours' drive from Riga by train, instead of wasting time and resources by transferring them to Kaiserwald.

The transfer process to the Kaiserwald Camp lasted several months and finally ended in October 1943.

July 1943

One evening in July 1943, with the improvement in the weather and arrival of spring, the building manager came and gathered us all in the yard. He informed us that he had received instruction to send us back to the ghetto and that he had no idea if we would come back to work in the building or not. We realized immediately that the relatively protected life in the building had ended for us. None of us said anything and everyone was left, as usual, with his thoughts to himself. For the first time in a long time we returned to the ghetto. I don't remember where we slept, but I don't think I slept at all that night.

Early the next morning, my father, Ze'eva and I, along with the other Jews who had worked in small working groups like us, reported with a heavy heart and full of fear to the entrance of the small ghetto. Jews who had been brought to the ghetto sometime earlier from Austria, Germany and the Netherlands, stood there with us. Each one of us was holding a small bundle with his few remaining possessions.

After a nerve-wracking wait, a few soldiers dressed in

uniforms of the Latvians' battalions who collaborated with the Germans, led by a German officer, ordered us to get organized in threes and start walking according to the soldiers' instructions.

Soon after we started walking, we realized that we were marching in a northeasterly direction. "At least it's not in the direction of Salaspils", I thought to myself. About two hours after we had started walking, we reached the Mežaparks area in the north of the city and within a short time we reached the gates of the Kaiserwald concentration camp. We had recently heard the name, but it was the first time we had actually seen it. They let us in and we found out that many Jews had already been brought there, most of them dressed in gray prison uniforms, some with stripes. The camp was full of people. The faces of many of them were lined with wrinkles, bearing the look of tired and desperate people, dragging their feet slowly as if without a purpose. My father, Ze'eva and I on the other hand, were in much better physical shape, although we were very scared for the new future that awaited us in this camp.

Within a short while we were ordered to report to an office building where every Jew who entered the gates of the camp was registered. There, we had a surprise. We saw my cousin Nyoma, the son of Uncle Lyuba. He was the first relative of the family that we'd seen since the end of November 1941, the eve of the first 'Action'. My father and Nyoma got together immediately, updated each other and stood together in line for registration. Ze'eva stood beside them and exchanged a few words with Nyoma as well. I was the youngest, and Nyoma only gave me a nod of the head 'hello' and I replied with a short welcome of my own.

My father reported first before the soldier who was registering the names, before me, before Ze'eva and before Nyoma. My father was asked to list his profession and field of expertise and said that he and the other family members (he made a gesture towards us with his hand), were all experts in carpentry and wood. We didn't know it then, but my father with his sharp survival instincts knew how to say the right thing in the right place, and thus prepared the next stage of our survival. The soldier raised his hand, instructing us to go in the direction where a group of Jews was already waiting. It turned out later that everyone had something in common: they all defined themselves as having a "useful" profession during registration.

The group of Jews to which we were assigned to join was sent to a specific building in the camp and we were ordered to wait there for further instructions. We spent the night there. We were woken up at four o'clock in the morning but we weren't told to do anything, so we just stayed in the building and waited.

After a few hours in which we still hadn't been given instructions, I decided to look around at the camp a little. While carefully wandering around, I got close a place that looked like an area for unloading trucks. I could see various types of trucks parked, other trucks were moving and a number of trucks had just arrived.

A few women dressed in prisoner clothes got off from one of the trucks that had arrived that moment. Something caught my attention. I looked at them again and to my amazement, among the women prisoners, I recognized Olga Rogalin from Libau, my childhood friend.

The Germans who had invaded Latvia from the south reached Liepaja (Libau), Olga's hometown, on 27.6.1941, even before reaching Riga. Olga's father, Joseph (Osip) Rogalin, was shot dead on the street on the same day. Olga and her mother, Zhenya, miraculously survived the 'Action' performed immediately afterwards and were sent to one of the satellite camps of the Kaiserwald camp, the VEF factory, the "women's factory" that employed only women who worked in winding electric coils used for radio and telephone equipment.

The VEF factory received its limited food supply from the big central camp - the Kaiserwald camp. For this purpose, every few days a supplies truck was sent, accompanied by a prisoner on duty, who loaded the equipment onto the truck. Olga was assigned to one of those trips.

I tried to get her attention, but I was afraid someone might notice my presence there, and I had neither reason nor permission to be there. Eventually she turned her face in my direction and saw me. I could see her eyes were sunken and filled with deep sadness. She looked at me and for a moment her eyes lit up. She motioned to me with her hand carefully and continued with the rest of the prisoners towards a building that looked like a food warehouse.

I got closer very cautiously to the same building and waited at the side, not far away from a group of Jews who were not all dressed in prisoners' uniform, and therefore I was inconspicuous. They were busy talking among themselves and didn't notice my presence. When Olga left the building, she saw me right away and approached me. She smiled sadly and asked me if I was alone in the camp, in other words asking who in our family had managed to survive until now. I gave her an update that my brother Ze'eva, my father and my cousin Nyoma were here with me and that all my other family members were gone. She updated me that her father was murdered and that she was in a women's camp named VEF with her mother Zhenya and that she was at the Kaiserwald camp as part of her turn of duty to accompany the delivery truck. Soon after, she told me she had to join the rest of the women who came with her and we said goodbye.

When I returned to the building where we spent the night, I found my father and Ze'eva, who gave me a questioning look, asking where I had been. I updated them about the trucks area, about meeting Olga Rogalin and about the content of our conversation. My father and Ze'eva looked at each other but didn't say a word.

I do not remember what else happened that day, but early the next morning the group of 'professionals' was ordered to prepare to leave the camp. A group of Latvians in German soldier uniform led us out of the camp. Again, a short while after we had started walking, we realized we were marching back to the city. As we approached the Daugava River near K. Valdemāra Street, I saw the Esplanāde to my left, the beautiful park close by and the Pilsetas Canal (Pilsētas Kanāls) where I used to play as a child and ski on the little hill with a sleigh. There were quite a few people there who had come to enjoy the beauty of the place in the spring. They lived in another world; the 'normal' world. At that moment, I felt the full force of our miserable existence and a heavy feeling of depression and hopelessness filled my heart.

We crossed the Daugava River and continued to walk in an easterly direction. At the end of this journey we reached the front gate of a textile factory, Lenta. We knew the place quite well, it wasn't far away from my father's factory, Zunde.

I instantly recognized the building built in stones that reminded me a little of the color of mustard, with a pair of long windows with round lintels above them as if they had been carved in the wall, and a row of four alcoves in the outer wall, also elongated.

Another stone structure rose above and behind that building in the shape of a high tower standing tall above all the surroundings. For a moment I felt relieved, but only for a moment. Within seconds we were taken inside the factory gates and found out that a labor camp had been built on the grounds of the factory and its buildings, with between 600 to 1,000 Jewish prisoners working at the time as forced laborers. Their number was diminishing over time.

***

The Commander of the Lenta camp was an SS officer named Fritz Scherwitz. Scherwitz turned Lenta into a large manufacturing facility for many different products and probably made a business of selling them privately for a personal profit. Scherwitz recruited Jewish craftsmen in many different ways to work in the Lenta camp. He was considered as one who protected 'his' Jews from being taken away from the Lenta camp and refrained from harassing them unnecessarily, as long as they worked effectively. At the same time, Scherwitz took care to be liked by his commanders so that they wouldn't interfere in his actions. SS officer Kurt Krause, the commander of the Riga ghetto and Scherwitz's deputy, Eduard Roschman, did not approve of Scherwitz's activities and tried to change the situation all the time, together with other SS officers. When Scherwitz was away from the Lenta camp, the prisoners were immediately treated worse. The battle between Scherwitz and Roschman continued for a long time.[9]

***

Within a short while I discovered that inside the Lenta camp, in the elongated wooden huts close to the surrounding high stone wall, the Germans had built a number of workshops - a sewing room, shoemakers' workshops, carpentry, and the like, which were intended to manufacture products for the use of the German officers stationed in Latvia. The Germans set up a team of about 200 Jews to work in those workshops. Thanks to the resourcefulness of my father, Ze'eva and I were sent along with him to work with the small team working in carpentry. Nyoma was assigned to work with another team.

I realized that I'd been downgraded from already poor status: from a maintenance worker who had no rights, I became a manual laborer with no rights. But again, the

---

9   Final Solution in Riga: Exploitation and Annihilation, 1941-1944, pp. 396-397.

knowledge and experience of my father with wood as raw material saved us for the time being.

Upon entering the Lenta camp, we were taken to one of the buildings that were used as a storage room. We received gray prisoner's uniforms, similar to the uniforms the prisoners in the Kaiserwald camp wore, but we were told not to wear them. Each of us received a number which replaced our previous identity and became our new name and image. This number accompanied us to the end of the War.

This warehouse became our sleeping area at night. In the evening, we would spread on the floor straw sacks that had been there when we'd arrived, and we would lie on top of them and fall asleep, exhausted. Every man took care of himself and my father who had always known how to get along, managed somehow to get us blankets. Every morning each one of us would roll up his blanket and take it with him to the carpentry and guard it 'with his life', otherwise it would be gone in an instant.

My father would get the manufacturing tasks from one of the German officers who came to visit the carpentry. Then he'd decide how to manufacture and distribute the tasks between the different carpenters on the team. I was often asked to perform the technical-related jobs, such as sanding the corners of the wooden products, painting the products, etc. Ze'eva, however, always found the easier jobs. I wasn't surprised; even before the War he didn't like manual labor. He was a man of books, knowledgeable in many ways, but he was not a worker; I didn't mind, because I loved manual labor. I enjoyed dealing with wood and I loved the smell of wood in the carpentry. I could feel the freshness coming from the logs that arrived at the carpentry from time to time. Each delivery had a different smell, depending on the type of wood and its origin. Dealing with wood gave me a warm, familiar, positive and comforting feeling.

The food we received was scarce, but at least it was given to us every day. We were constantly guarded, but our guards didn't really bother us. From time to time, German officers came for inspections and before any such inspection, we were required to wear the prisoners' uniforms we'd received. After the inspection, we'd go back to wearing the clothes we had. We did not feel safe for a moment, and we knew that new trouble could fall upon us at any time.

There were rumors, as usual. Countless rumors, strange and bizarre, most of them depressing, that the Germans conquered Moscow and Leningrad, that the Germans had made a decision to exterminate all remaining Jews in Riga including us, and many more. Those rumors only contributed to the large sense of insecurity in our lives.

Compared to other German officers who served as commanders of camps where I'd been, one might say that Scherwitz, the commander of the Lenta camp, had tried to at least be more human than others. For example, he would sometimes taste the food prepared for the prisoners to see if it was edible. A human gesture so small and humble, but seemed particularly outstanding under the circumstances.

CHAPTER SEVEN

PARTING FROM ZE'EVA
October 1943 - October 1944

Several months went by until October 1943.

One day in October 1943, the camp commander called all the adults, including my father, to gather in the corner of the courtyard of the camp. My father immediately reported. In the distance, I could see the camp commander talking, waving his hands and pointing to some imaginary point outside the camp. Even from a distance, it was clear that the news was bad. The adults' faces became ashen, my father's face, too, his shoulders slumped and his arm supporting his lowered head. I was afraid to approach him. I wanted another minute of grace, of not knowing. My father came over and told me to fetch Ze'eva as soon as possible.

When Ze'eva came, my father took us aside and told us that the Germans had decided to send 150 people from our camp, to another labor camp in Courland (Courland Peninsula is actually the south-western part of Latvia). The camp Commander had told them that it was a labor camp where the work was very difficult, the conditions were tough and only the strong prisoners should be sent there - not the adults like my father, but those who were twenty and thirty-years-old, because they were the only ones who had a chance of surviving there.

In a deep and slow voice, my father let us know that he was instructed to send one of his sons on that shipment. Then he told both of us that he had decided that Ze'eva would be the one to join that shipment and I, the younger one, would stay with him.

I don't know what went through my father's mind in those moments, why did he choose Ze'eva and not me, and what he was feeling, but I didn't ask. My father didn't offer an explanation either. Ze'eva was a very spiritual person, with a character of a philosopher; had he survived the War, he most probably would have studied philosophy. I, on the other hand, was a practical man. I loved working with my hands and I was also physically strong. In my view, I was as strong as Ze'eva, although he was older than me. But in that situation, the continued day-to-day struggle for existence and survival, where my father's experience and wisdom managed to save us, there was neither the time nor the energy to question my father's decision. He decided and that was it.

He ordered Ze'eva to collect his belongings and report at the assembly point of that group. Ze'eva looked at my father and me and left us without a word. **This was the last time my father and I ever saw him**.

After the War we found out that the place where that labor camp had been set up was called Dundaga (kurzeme seelager) and the prisoners in that camp logged trees. The tree logging was done under appalling working conditions: freezing cold, almost no food, hard physical work, and no medication or any other means to deal with illness and injuries.

The life expectancy of the prisoners working there was minimal and many of them had died while working. It was, in fact, an extermination camp by the means of forced labor, which was directed by SS soldiers.

The atrocities committed against the Jews in that extermination camp were described in a book called "So it was indeed" by Abraham Shpungin. One of the stories in the book speaks of the solution the camp commander found for the many bodies that had accumulated in the camp during the harsh winter. Since the land was frozen and the dead could not be buried, the commander gave an order to drill a hole through the ice covering the Baltic Sea and to throw the bodies into the hole. When spring came and the ice melted, the bodies were washed ashore and this is how people learned about the horror.

We also found out that during his stay in Dundaga, Ze'eva became sick with tuberculosis and pneumonia and was sent by truck, along with other patients, to the Kaiserwald camp. In an amazing coincidence, that truck arrived to the Kaiserwald camp and began to unload its human cargo at the same time as Olga Rogalin, my childhood friend, arrived there with a delivery truck that was sent from the women's VEF camp, just as she had arrived on the day I met her there.

When the delivery truck arrived in the parking lot near the infirmary and the supplies room, Olga recognized Ze'eva among the prisoners that were downloaded from a truck parked nearby and taken to the infirmary. When she asked, she was told that it was a truck that brought sick prisoners from some labor camp. When Olga was able to get closer to Ze'eva, she saw that he was in terrible physical condition and seemed to be on his deathbed. He lay sprawled on the floor at the entrance to the infirmary along with others, his senses vague. Olga made eye contact with him and carefully motioned with her hand that she could see him. Ze'eva shook himself momentarily from the unconsciousness that he had been in and they managed to exchange a few words. Ze'eva told her that he was coming from Dundaga labor camp. Olga asked one of the prisoners who worked in the infirmary whom she had met on a previous occasion when she came with the supply truck and begged that a doctor examine Ze'eva. He heeded her request and miraculously, a Jewish doctor who also worked as a prisoner in the infirmary, came and checked Ze'eva. It was a short medical check and at the end of it he told Olga and the prisoner who mediated between them, "He is lost, he has but a few hours to live", and left.

Olga subsequently requested the prisoner who worked in the infirmary to separate Ze'eva from the rest of the sick prisoners and keep an eye on him. She promised to compensate him, although she had no idea how she would do it.

A few days later, Olga was able to volunteer herself to the escort mission of the supply vehicles and arrived at the Kaiserwald camp, but Ze'eva was gone.

She found the prisoner that had helped her on her previous visit and asked him what had happened to Ze'eva. The answer was that Ze'eva, along with the rest of the sick people, was sent to his death in an extermination camp called Auschwitz. He was 22-years-old when he died.

I found out about the encounter between Olga and Ze'eva in the infirmary of the Kaiserwald camp only several years after the War, after I came to the land of Israel and Olga found the courage and strength to tell me about it. Only then I was able to fully understand and accept the certainty of Ze'eva's death and the understanding that all hope was lost and I would never see my brother Ze'eva again.

With great sadness, I hurried to tell my father (who had come the land of Israel two years before me). My father's answer shocked me. He looked at me with a sad look and told me with a straight face, "I have known that for years, I just never told you." He continued and said, "While we were in the Lenta labor camp, someone handed me a note in Olga Rogalin's handwriting and the note said: *Ze'eva was sent to Auschwitz, together with all the patients who were in the infirmary of the Kaiserwald camp*". I didn't tell you about it so as not to upset you." My father's words shocked me. I couldn't figure out how he'd got his hands on this note. How many hands had that note passed through on the way? How was I not aware of it when we were in the Lenta camp? But my father didn't provide any answers and my questions remained unanswered.

My father and I stayed in the Lenta camp another year, until October 1944, after parting from Ze'eva.

June 2010

Assa and I visited Riga again in June 2010. We wanted to visit other milestones in our father's survival journey like we had on our previous visit. This time we decided to visit the Lenta factory. We boarded a bus from the Central Bus Station in Riga, a short walking distance from the central city market. The bus's route took us through a bus station on the other side of the Daugava River. While sitting on the bus and looking out the window at the view on the bridge crossing the river, I gave an update to Assa about our father's story and the time he spent in Lenta. Assa listened quietly until I reached the description of the parting from Ze'eva. He interrupted and asked, "What do you mean he just went?" He said it in such a loud voice that all the passengers sitting next to us heard him. "They didn't have some sort of farewell gesture? They didn't have any kind of farewell, words of goodbye, a hug, something?" he asked. "Not that I know of", I replied. "From what I understood from Dad, the event was very quick and under a continuous sense of existential threat, it was no place to show emotions", I added. "I must see the yard where they were separated forever", said Assa and became very quiet.

Even before we reached the bus station, we knew we had arrived. We couldn't miss the tall building my father had told me about. Not only that, but there was a clear turquoise sign at the entrance bordered by a white line, on which it was clearly written 'Lenta' and below it, 'Anno 1880'. We had arrived.

We walked towards the entrance gate that was wide open with a stone structure at its side where a guard was sitting. Directly in front of us we saw the building my father had told me about. It was impossible to be mistaken. We faced a building with a pair of elongated windows and a circular lintel, above which we saw the same series of four alcoves in the exterior wall. Behind the building, another stone structure was indeed rising high. We realized that we were seeing the same image our father had seen when he arrived at the Lenta camp. Standing just in front of the lower structure, we saw a large wooden structure painted green. Our father hadn't said anything about it, but it seemed as if it had been there for many years. We made a note to ask him about it upon our return.

Between the entrance gate and the green structure, we recognized the square our father had spoken about. It was rectangular, about twenty meters wide and one hundred and fifty meters long. On one side, the square ended with the fence of the plant. On the other side, the square ended with elongated industrial halls, each hall two-stories high with large gaping windows on the second floor. These were apparently the halls my father had told me about, or halls that had been built on top of the wooden shacks my father mentioned. Indeed, almost nothing had changed in the factory; it remained as it was.

The guard came out from the gatehouse and made signs that we could not enter. Assa and I looked at each other and without saying a word, divided tasks between us. I would keep the guard busy and he would use the time to photograph the place and the square near the gate.

I went to the guard and tried talking to him in English, but he motioned immediately that he didn't understand a word and answered in Latvian. I didn't need to speak Latvian to understand what he was saying; his tone made it clear that entry was forbidden. I remembered that I had an English Latvian dictionary in my bag. I took it out and with the guard's help, and the use of body language and a medley of English, German and Russian (I don't speak Russian and I can understand only a few words in German) I tried to explain that our grandfather and our father worked here in the past and that we simply wanted to see the place. To my surprise he understood, and the expression on his face turned softer.

He answered - or at least this is what I understood - that the factory owner was currently on a plane, or had been on a plane, or will be on a plane, on her way to Germany or on her way from Germany, and without her approval, we weren't allowed to enter the plant. Out of the corner of my eye I saw that Assa was still taking photographs and hadn't yet finished.

I kept the guard busy for a few more minutes until Assa returned. I thanked the guard. We walked out the entrance gate and started walking along the stone wall surrounding the plant. About forty-five minutes later, we finished circling the plant, walking slowly. From the back of the plant we were able to see the same industrial halls where our father had worked and slept at night with his father and brother Ze'eva, and we saw the tall stone tower.

It was a strange feeling to look at the silent stone walls, which had witnessed a part of the survival journey of our father and grandfather. But to my surprise, I didn't feel any sense of excitement or awe from the sight. All I saw was old stone walls wrapped in a thick layer of dirt. For Assa, however, it seemed as though being in the same square where our father and Ze'eva had been separated for the last time left some sediment and sadness in him. We waited for the bus and went back to town.

The Lenta plant, 2010

CHAPTER EIGHT

FROM THE LENTA CAMP TO THE STUTTHOF AND BURGGRABEN CAMPS IN GERMANY
1944

Meanwhile, at the forefront of the fighting, the Russian army had begun being victorious in the battle against the German army and started pushing it west, beyond the limits of the Soviet Union and even further. The Germans realized that it was only a matter of time before the world found out about the massacres committed against the Jewish population that was under their control. Therefore, during 1944 the Germans began a new campaign, the campaign for the elimination of evidence of the atrocities committed, in Latvia as well.

In April 1944, groups of Jewish prisoners were sent to dig out the bodies of their slaughtered brothers from death pits across the country and burn them. The German ground the remains of the bodies using special machinery. Jews who were engaged in that terrible job were killed immediately after.

On October 6, 1944, the Red Army advanced westward and crossed the border between Russia and Latvia. They entered Latvia and broke the communication lines between the German army in Latvia and the rest of the German army that had been deployed south of Latvia. The Germans began to evacuate the soldiers and their families, the collaborators and all the equipment they had looted during their stay in Latvia to Germany by sea, using ships. At one point, they began to evacuate the prisoners in the Kaiserwald concentration camp to the forced labor camp Stutthof, established near the city of Danzig in Germany (near the city of Gdansk in today's Poland).

As the Russian army approached the city of Riga itself, the Germans began to transfer all Jewish prisoners, including those who were in the Lenta camp, by sea, to the Stutthof concentration camp. The Jewish prisoners whom the Germans had a reason to believe could not survive the journey to the Stutthof concentration camp were shot on the spot.

Until 1942, prisoners had been brought to the Stutthof concentration camp by truck. After 1942, due to expansion of the camp, the prisoners were gathered in the province cities from which they were sent to Stutthof by truck or electric tram to a place where they were loaded onto a train that ran all the way to the small railway station in the village of Stutthof.

However, the prisoners arriving at the Stutthof camp during 1944 from the Baltic countries, Estonia, Latvia and Lithuania, had done so via barges or freight boats sailing to Danzig, and from there by truck or cargo train to that train station in the village of Stutthof.

Sorting of the prisoners took place at the railway station. The men were loaded on trains and usually sent to Germany, and the women and children were sent to Stutthof. After the prisoners had been registered, they were sent to a quarantine that lasted between two and four weeks. The prisoners were supposed to receive a daily food ration of between 1,800 to 2,000 calories. But in reality, the prisoners were given a daily ration that didn't even reach 1,000 calories. Many prisoners were sick with typhus.

Prisoners were murdered in the Stutthof camp every day. The amount of bodies was so great that the crematorium couldn't keep up with the rate of cremation.[10]

October 1944

Autumn of 1944 arrived and the evenings were already very cold. We felt it in our bones through our poor clothing. More than three years had passed since the entry of the Germans, the destruction of our world and the disappearance of Mother and Robby from our lives. A year had passed since we were separated from Ze'eva and my father had not said a single word on the subject and I never asked. I didn't have to. We hadn't heard anything from Ze'eva and I figured out that he, too, was lost. But until it was proven otherwise, he was still alive in my mind.

The rumor rate has increased. The rumors now said that the Germans were losing, the Russians were winning and that the evacuation of prisoners from the Kaiserwald camp had begun. Other rumors claimed that prisoners from the Kaiserwald camp were actually being killed. This time, the rumors had some results. There were several attempts

---

10   The Final Solution in Riga: Exploitation and Annihilation, 1941-1944, p 420.

by Jewish prisoners to escape from Lenta. One morning we found out that my cousin Nyoma Gutkin and his friend Chone Glazer had also fled from the camp! Several days passed and we didn't hear that he had been caught.

Chone, who worked in the sewing shop, made some German officer's clothes for himself and offered to sew the same clothing for Nyoma too, but Nyoma refused. At the end of one of the working days, Nyoma and Chone took advantage of the lack of attention of the guards, jumped over the fence of the Lenta camp and went out to the street nearby. They rushed off toward the bridge crossing the Daugava River in order to return into the city of Riga itself. When they got close to the bridge, they chose to split: Nyoma went on one side of the bridge and Chone went, dressed in a German officer's clothes, on the other side of the bridge. Chone had the misfortune that a car with German officers passed by. The passengers were surprised to see a German officer crossing the bridge on foot. They stopped beside him to offer him a lift. Apparently, they quickly recognized that he was a prisoner disguised as a German officer and they shot and killed him on the spot. Nyoma, however, continued walking on the other side of the bridge. With amazing self-control, he completely ignored what was happening on the other side of the road, crossed the bridge and disappeared between the houses of the old town of Riga.

After the War, I met Nyoma and he told me that before he moved to the ghetto, he found a Latvian shoemaker who agreed to hide him in exchange for money that was paid partly as an advance, with the balance to be paid when

Nyoma arrived to hide at his place. Indeed, after fleeing from the Lenta camp, Nyoma arrived at the shoemaker's place. The shoemaker kept his part of the bargain and hid Nyoma for many months, until the Russian army entered Riga.

The Russians were approaching Riga. This was no longer a rumor; it was almost common knowledge. One evening in October 1944, all the prisoners in the Lenta camp, including my father and myself, received an order to report in the square in front of the camp the next morning. We had a feeling just like the feeling we had when we left the building in no. 30 Ģertrūdes Street. We realized that the period we'd spent in the Lenta camp had ended for us and again this did not bode well. At least this time it didn't come as a surprise. As usual, my father said nothing and neither did I. Each of us was left with his own thoughts.

A new rumor quickly circulated among the prisoners in the camp. One of the German soldiers guarding the camp said that they were taking us to Germany the next day. One version of that rumor was that the destination was Hamburg; another version was that the destination was Berlin.

The next morning, my father and I reported in the square in front of the camp, once again each holding a small bundle in his hand with his few belongings. Many other prisoners reported together with us. The guards immediately started yelling at us in German to stand in threesomes. After that, we each received some food and the Germans began marching us toward the Daugava River, not far from the camp.

When we reached the river, we saw five barges, usually used to transport freights on the river. Each barge was 30-40 meters long with a flat floor and about 2-meter-high walls, which formed a shallow bath. Each barge had a large rudder at the edge and was tied by a cable to a tugboat.

The barges stood side by side. On some of the barges there were a few German soldiers and other prisoners from the camp who were busy loading boxes with various equipment parts. The guards divided us into groups of about 80 prisoners each and ordered our group to go to one of the barges. We sat on the floor of the barge. Almost two hours later we heard the engine of the tugboat starting and after a few moments we felt the cable between our barge and the tugboat tighten, and our barge started moving toward the center of the river.

While the tugboat moved slowly in the river, I saw from my seat that we were sailing in the direction of the outlet to the sea. Now I understood that the rumors from last night had an element of truth in them, they were really taking us to Germany - and by sailing, which I hated.

The journey took five days and it was not a pleasure cruise! The Baltic Sea was an area plagued with submarines. Many German ships were sunk and thousands plunged into the depths of the Baltic Sea. The sea was rough and our barge rocked, but despite all my efforts to remember, I still don't remember throwing up even once during that journey.

Only two of the five barges survived the journey. Our barge was one of them. The other three were sunk by the Russians or simply overturned into the rough sea.

The sailing ended when we arrived on the shore somewhere, not at any formal port. The guards who escorted us ordered us to get off the barge and sit on the beach. It was a relief, because I was happy to feel the solid ground beneath my feet again.

We lay on the beach throughout the day and during the night, without any food or drink except for what was left from the food we had received when we'd left Lenta camp. We were exhausted. The next morning, our second day on the beach, a truck full of soldiers arrived. They got off the truck and immediately began yelling at us in German to get up, stand in threesomes and be ready to walk. We began a long walk on a foreign and hostile land. I realized that from now on, my knowledge of German and my father's limited knowledge too would be absolutely essential. After what felt like endless walking, we arrived at a terrible place: the Stutthof concentration camp.

We stayed there for three days, during which we didn't get anything to eat at all, and got to drink only once - filthy muddy water which we drank thirstily under the constant yelling from our German guards. Those were three bad days and I don't remember anything except that we were subjected to continuous inspections, unceasing physical and verbal abuse including lashes to the many prisoners that were there, the hunger and the thirst. The place was full of prisoners in prison uniforms, looking terrified and on the verge of death.

Three days after our arrival to Stutthof, a few of the prisoners who had come with us from Riga were gathered, including us. We were teamed up with another group of prisoners and marched away. The feeling was that wherever we were going, the situation couldn't possibly be any worse than that in the Stutthof camp, only better. The other prisoners told us that in the condition we'd arrived to the Stutthof concentration camp in, we wouldn't have survived a week.

This journey took two days non-stop. Some of the prisoners collapsed during the walk and were shot at once. At the end of this long journey, my father and I arrived at the Burggraben camp, which was a sub-camp of the Stutthof camp system, in a suburb known today by the name Kokoszki, of the polish city Gdansk. My father and I were housed in a barracks residence of forced labor prisoners. As newcomers, we both got a bunk in the second bunk's floor, which we had to share with another thirty prisoners.

The very next day after our arrival to the Burggraben camp, we marched five kilometers, escorted by Polish and Ukrainian guards dressed in German uniforms and holding loaded guns, until we reached the gates of a large factory. We arrived at a shipyard by the name of Schichau, where German submarines were manufactured. My father and I were sent to a big industrial hall with a lot of machinery. We were teamed up as assistants to a Polish welder, a forced labor prisoner himself. The task of our team, which consisted of six prisoners, was to pick up iron plates and hold them together with similar iron plates held by other prisoners, so that both plates could be welded together. These plates were used in building submarines in the shipyard. The Polish welder would talk to us in Polish and using our knowledge of Russian we had learnt to understand the few commands he would give us, commands that were needed to do the job.

The work was carried out in two shifts of 12 hours each, day and night, without a break. We were fortunate that we had been assigned to the day shift on a regular basis, so that every night we returned to camp.

Whenever my father or I were asked to go to a different area of the plant we tried to do it together, in order not to be separated.

The amount of food supplied to us each day was very small, and the food itself was very dull - one bowl of diluted soup a day; so diluted that it was basically water. It turned out that the food shortage was a mirror image of the situation at the German front. In the beginning, when the Germans were succeeding on the Russian front one battle after the other, and advanced deeper into Soviet territory, food was reasonably available. The vast agricultural areas of Russia were a source of food to the Germans, and the Jewish slave laborers, like us, enjoyed fair food rations. As the German situation at the front and the hinterland deteriorated, so did the food rations assigned to the slave laborers.

Before long, the result could be seen - we all weakened. Our forces dwindled. Dysentery and typhus raised their heads and beat us mercilessly. Pretty soon it wasn't enough for six prisoners to lift the iron plate and more prisoners were needed for each working team to successfully pick them up. By the end, we hardly had the strength to walk back the five kilometers that separated the Camp from the shipyard. At this point we knew it was just a short matter of time until we couldn't keep walking to the shipyard and would be unable to work. The implication was clear: being shot to death.

In addition, all instructions from the German guards were given in German. Whoever didn't understand the guards and couldn't follow the orders was shot immediately. Without a doubt, the fact that my father and I understood German helped us to survive.

Since our arrival at the Burggraben camp, we knew nothing about what was happening on the war front. We were completely isolated and cut off from all information, until the day we faintly heard the sound of cannon fire from far away. The rumor was that these were the sounds of the Russian army's cannon fire. That day, for the first time, I realized that the war front was getting closer, the Russians were finally winning and the chance that we would be released from the Germans was increasing.

This piece of news was the only thing that still gave us hope and kept us going. Each of us felt that if he could only survive another day and yet another day, he might live to see the Russians save him before he died of exhaustion. That was the motto. After three and a half years as prisoners, we'd learned not to plan ahead. All we wanted was to survive the current day. It dictated the so little we could control, and that was the only horizon we could imagine.

In retrospect, we were lucky that we were sent to the sub-camp of Burggraben, because the remaining prisoners in the Stutthof main camp were not as fortunate.

I learned from Kaufman's book that as early as January 1945, a lot of the prisoners were executed and the Germans led the remaining prisoners on horrible death marches. The mortality rate in those marches was very high, especially among the Jewish women prisoners. It is estimated that out of

22,500 prisoners who were evacuated by foot, 12,000 prisoners, about 10,000 of which were Jews, it was mostly women who had died. After their departure, 33,948 people were left in the Stutthof camp complex, including 11,863 in the Stutthof camp itself and the rest in the sub-camps, including the Burggraben camp. Among them was my father and I.

On February 10, 1945 the Germans assembled a group of Jewish prisoners who were with us in the Burggraben camp and began marching them outside the camp. I found out later that the Germans had taken them on a death march toward a town named Lauenburg and many of them died or were shot on the way.

CHAPTER NINE

LIBERATION: THE RETURN TO RIGA AND THE DECISION TO IMMIGRATE TO THE LAND OF ISRAEL

March 1945

On March 22, 1945, almost 4 years (46 months) after the Germans had entered Riga, my father had lost all his strength. He was suffering from typhus or dysentery and had already lost more than half of his body weight and no longer had the strength to work. The implication was obvious. As soon as the work teams left for work and the Germans performed the count, they'd find out that my father was left in the barracks and he would be executed immediately. I tried to convince him to come out with me, but he was finished. Nothing was left from the same heavy built, smiling and self-confident man he was before the Germans invaded Latvia and entered Riga. The loss of his wife and two of his children, the hard work, the terrible hunger and loss of faith in surviving his life as a prisoner overwhelmed him. He lay on his bunk on the second bunk floor and refused to get up and climb down from his high bunk to the floor. Having no choice, I had to leave him there and report to the square along with the other work teams headed for the shipyard. I was convinced that when I got back at the end of the day, my father would no longer be there.

But my father and I were lucky again. After leaving from the Burggraben camp toward the shipyard, the camp was bombed by the Russian army's artillery. The shells exploded around the camp and drove the German guards who were there at the time to hiding places, where they remained for a long time.

One of the shells hit the barracks where my father was left, penetrated through the roof of the barracks, passed through the stories of bunks near the bunk he lay on and exploded on the floor of the barracks. The fact that his bunk was on the second bunk floor, which made life difficult for him, actually saved his life. My father was only wounded by shrapnel in his legs. The German guards didn't even bother to check if anyone was left alive in the barracks or not. My father was left dazing on the bunk until I came back that night and found him in serious medical condition, but alive.

All that night I talked to him and prevented him from losing consciousness. The feeling was that we were really close to the end of the nightmare, and that the Russian army was so close, that it was only a matter of a few days until we would be released and the ones who could survive until then would be saved.

Early in the morning on the following day, March 23, 1945, we discovered that the German guards had disappeared and left us alone. We were left lying slumped on our bunks. We didn't have the strength to escape and anyway, we had nowhere to escape to. Unfortunately, some of our colleagues, prisoners in the barracks, didn't make it and died in those same hours.

Later in the morning of that day, a convoy of Russian army military vehicles broke down the Burggraben camp gate! **We were free! We were saved!**

Among the Russian army soldiers who entered the camp on the first convoy of vehicles was a Jewish doctor named Fleischmann. He joined the other Russian soldiers who began walking around the barracks and helping the prisoners, human skeletons, to leave the buildings for the first time in years, as free men.

He came to our barracks and entered after all the occupants had left, except for my father, myself and a number of prisoners who were in the same condition as my father. He turned to me and asked me in Russian who I was and where I was from. Something in his accent drew my father's attention. Feebly, my father answered in Yiddish, "We are from Riga, we are Jewish, and they killed us." I was amazed when the doctor looked at my father and replied in Yiddish, in a trembling voice, "I am also a Jew from Riga and I already know that they killed all the Jews. You are the first Jews I've met." Dr. Fleischman ordered two soldiers to bring a stretcher, help my father down from the bunk and put him on the stretcher. We left our barracks to a new reality, my father lying on a stretcher carried by two Russian soldiers followed by Dr. Fleischmann, and finally me at the end, physically exhausted, hungry, but walking straight on my own two feet. **After all**

that, the Germans and their Latvian collaborators, damn them, did not manage to kill me.

Dr. Fleischman ordered the stretcher-bearers to put my father in an army truck, into which I also climbed, and we were taken to a hospital run by the Russian army near the city of Danzig. In the first few days my father was still in very bad condition and I wasn't sure that he would survive. My own state was pretty bad. After months of constant hunger I was very weak, with bruised hands and I was tired, very tired. Although I felt the relief that followed the dramatic change in our situation, the trauma I had endured in recent years depressed me, and the uncertainty about our future put a burden on me too. But my body strengthened day by day. Even my father's condition started improving and he even began to smile from time to time. As our bodies strengthened, so was our mood improved. Within a few days, my father was getting out of bed and trying to walk in the room. We slowly started to expand the scope of our tours and eventually we found that we'd been touring throughout the day around the entire hospital.

Dr. Fleischmann, the Jewish doctor who took care of us so well came to visit my father once more and then disappeared, without me being able to thank him. I have no idea what happened to him.

We spent two months in the military hospital. We received medical treatment and food, which helped our bodies and spirits to recover. At the end of those two months we received an order from one of the Russian officers at the hospital to evacuate and move to a transit camp near the city of Danzig, which had previously served as a German army camp. More survivors from the labor camps and German extermination camps were relocated to that transit camp until it was decided what to do with them. Only after the meeting with the other survivors in the transit camp did I learn for the first time the extent of the horrors of the extermination camps and the mass murder of Jews all over Europe.

No one in the Russian army knew what to do with us and none of them even bothered to take care of us. We were supposed to take care of ourselves, including finding our own food. Fortunately, good-hearted Russian soldiers let us eat from their food rations. There was no future in staying in the transit camp, so my father and I decided to try and return to Riga. And so using Russian military trains moving east, and hitchhiking with military trucks traveling from city to city moving equipment and supplies, we did.

München-Freimann 1946   Riga. Silvester 1940/41

Samuel Gutkin, before and after WW II

June 1945

We arrived in Riga in June 1945, exactly four years after the Germans invaded Latvia. I was 16-years-old when the Germans arrived in Riga and I returned to Riga a 20-year-old young man; a completely different person. Even Riga was a different city than the one I'd grown up in - not the joyful and beautiful city I knew as a child, but a drab and sad city, who's people frightened and very careful about what they said and did due to the Communist regime. But apart from that, there was no sign of the Holocaust of the Jews who had lived in Riga before the German army invaded Latvia. Life went on as usual, as if nothing happened.

My father was no longer the man he was when I was a child. He didn't convert back into the confident master he was on the eve of the Russians entrance to Latvia in June 1940, but a man whose sadness and exhaustion from life were evident in his eyes and face. His vitality, which was so characteristic of him, had disappeared completely. But his practical nature remained. As a matter of fact, that same day he found us a place to live: a couple of rooms in a six-room apartment not far from the big building that was our home until the eve of the War.

The next day, my father and I went to visit Mr. Blumberges at home, to check what had happened to the valuables and the other things that he had been safe-keeping for us since the eve of moving to the ghetto four years earlier.

To our great disappointment, we realized that in order to survive during the War, Mr. Blumberges and his wife had sold all the valuables left in his safe, including the silver cutlery and the pictures, which we had counted on. We didn't need the other stuff. In a spur of the moment decision, my father chose to leave them with the couple out of gratitude for them giving my father an early warning when the Nazis entered Riga - a warning that had saved our lives.

We decided we had no choice but to check whether anything was left in the hiding place my father had prepared in our apartment during the days before moving to the ghetto. Until that moment, we hadn't been close to the big building at all. We walked towards the building and when I stood in front of the large, impressive building for the first time in four years, I felt sick to my stomach. I remembered the evening we'd left our apartment along with my mother, Robby and Ze'eva, towards a very tragic future. My father's face showed nothing, blank of any emotion. Outside, nothing had changed; there was nothing to suggest that a tragedy had happened to some of the previous residents. I did see one change: at the entrance to the courtyard from Brivibas Street stood a Russian soldier that stopped strangers from entering the courtyard and the apartments in the different entrances. My father went up to him and asked if he could enter, but the guard refused to allow us in and said that the building, including all its entrances, was now a military area where officers of the Russian army lived. "I lived in an apartment on the first floor before the War", my father told the guard, "I only wish to look at it for a moment and then I'll leave", he added. It worked. The guard allowed us to enter the courtyard and we went up to the rear entrance of the apartment.

We climbed the stairs to the apartment that led to what was once a warm and protected home, before the destruction of my entire world. Now I had mixed feelings about it. We got to the first floor and my father went to the door of the apartment and knocked on it. An elderly woman opened the door and asked us what we wanted. "My name is Samuel Gutkin", my father said, "I lived in this apartment before the War. I'm here with my son Max, may we come in?" "Certainly", the woman said, and immediately offered us a cup of tea. We accepted gladly and went into the apartment's living room, which was so familiar to me.

The living room walls still bore the wallpaper my mother had pasted on it before my Bar Mitzvah dinner party. I couldn't resist, and I went to the wall and unconsciously stroked the wallpaper, as if to feel my mother's touch. I saw through the corner of my eye that our hostess had seen me do it, but she said nothing. In the living room there was an unfamiliar table and a number of chairs that our host beckoned us to sit on as she turned towards the kitchen.

A few minutes later, an older man came out of one of the rooms, dressed in a Russian military uniform. His wife had already managed to update him about our presence. He joined us and asked us again for our name. My father told him our family name in Russian and then our host told us, his emotions clearly showing in his voice, that he was a Jew and his wife was Jewish too, that he served in the Russian Army as a doctor and he got this beautiful apartment because of that status.

We didn't have to explain to them that my father and I

were the only ones remaining in our entire family; they could figure it out by themselves. Both were very pleasant and the conversation flowed. At some point, when my father felt comfortable and confident enough with this Jewish couple, he told them why we had come. "In the days preceding our deportation to the ghetto, I hid my late wife's jewelry in one of the walls here. It has great sentimental value for me and I would like to take it out and take it with me." They looked at each other and the doctor replied cordially, "We are about to leave the house, we're going out for a day or two. When we return, the apartment should be clean. We don't know anything", and told us where to leave the key to the apartment. We waited until the benevolent couple moved out and my father went to the hiding place. He began peeling the wallpaper from the corner of the wall using his hand, grabbed the unattached brick and pulled it out. For a moment I felt the tension of not knowing what was in there, but only for a moment. All the jewelry, photos and gold coins my father had hidden in the box were there, just as he left them. We put them in our clothes, left the apartment and put the key in the place they'd instructed us to.

In the days of the Soviet harsh rule, it was a great danger to be caught in town with such property. Therefore, we hurried back to our rented rooms, hoping we wouldn't get caught on our way with the valuable possessions we carried in our clothes. Once we'd returned, my father hid the jewels and the gold coins again.

Only when I'd returned to Riga did I realize the extent of the destruction and the size of the horror that we, the Jews, had suffered. The city disturbed me and reminded of my mother and my lost brothers constantly.

I knew it was only a matter of time before I would leave the city, although it was highly dangerous because the government had banned movement out of the city without a permit, and anyone caught trying to cross the border outside of the new USSR was in danger of being killed. I wasn't afraid of death. In fact, I wasn't afraid of anything. Nothing could be worse than what I had gone through in the last four years. I wanted to go to the land of Israel and I was willing to take the risk to do so.

I started working in a factory during the day and in the evenings I went to night school to complete a high school diploma, but all my resources were devoted to leaving Latvia in general and Riga in particular.

One evening I spoke to my father about it and I found out that he felt the same and was ready to take the risk of trying to cross the border In an attempt to eventually get to the land of Israel. He had acquaintances there, the founders of the LAIMA Factory, who were smart enough to emigrate from Latvia to the land of Israel before the Russian invasion. He believed that they, along with the descendants of the Schalman couple who had perished in the first Action, who were living in the land of Israel, would be able to help him rebuild his life again.

Very carefully I started to snoop around among the Jews my age I had met over time in the city, about the possibility of crossing the border. That was when I first learned about the Jewish organization 'HaBrichah' (The Escape) that helped Jews escape from the Soviet Union and come to the land of

Israel. As far as I can recall, back then I also met Tanya, the sister of Isia Schlossberg who had taught me Latvian 11 years before. She told me that Isia got drafted by the Russian army and didn't return, so it was assumed that he was probably killed during the War.

CHAPTER TEN

THE JOURNEY TO THE LAND OF ISRAEL

1946 - 1948

In the spring of 1946 my father and I met secretly with representatives of 'HaBrichah' and made plans with them to cross the Latvian border towards Poland and from there, to the American zone in Germany. We paid them in advance in gold coins we had collected from the hiding place in the apartment and we prepared to leave.

One day we received a notice that we had to leave that night. We loaded the few belongings we had in two suitcases and reported at the appointed time and place we were told. We met with other Jews gathered there for the same purpose: to escape from the Soviet Union and come to the land of Israel. The 'Brichah' representatives arrived with a truck and drove us to the border crossing point. We walked for many hours until we reached a railroad. There we had to hide in the vegetation around the railroad until the next night. The next night, a short train came out of nowhere carrying freight cars. The train stopped next to us and other representatives of the 'Brichah' got out and signaled us to get on. We traveled for more than a day on that train, which periodically stopped at different stations, until we reached the end of the journey, the city of Lodge in Poland. In Lodge, we were transferred to a building where all the Jewish refugees who used the services of the 'Brichah' to leave Europe and come to the land of Israel, were brought.

During our stay at the Lodge building, we found out that Olga and her mother Zhenya Rogalin were still alive and were also staying in Lodge. We looked for them and ultimately found them in another building that was also used by the 'Brichah' for Jewish refugees. The joyfulness of that meeting was mixed with great sadness, but for the first time since the War ended, I felt a sense of family warmth again. It was clear that we would spend time together until we were transferred to the next station in our escape route.

During this waiting period, my father and Zhenya, Olga's mother, decided to get married and to try rebuild the rest of their lives together. As a result, Olga Rogalin, my childhood friend and I, became stepbrother and stepsister.

A month after our arrival in Lodge, representatives of the 'Brichah' helped us smuggle through the Polish border and get to the American zone in Berlin and from there to Munich, in southern Germany.

When we arrived in Munich, a surprise awaited us. We found out that Nyoma Gutkin, the son of my late Uncle Lyuba was also in the city. Since he'd escaped from the Lenta camp we'd had no information about what had happened to him. After we met, I tried to talk to him about his experiences, but he didn't want to share much. All he told me about was the escape from the Lenta camp, the death of Chone, hiding with the Latvian shoemaker and how immediately upon the entry of the Russians to Riga, he escaped to Germany and eventually came to Munich like us. However, he spent a lot of time with my father. I think they were talking about financial matters, but this is only speculation.

I lived with friends of my father in Munich and worked in the UNRWA[11] camp as a driver. On Saturdays and Sundays we worked for the 'Brichah' and we drove Jews to Austria. From there the Jews would cross the Alps to Italy.

In February 1947 I began my own journey to the land of Israel. We traveled by foot through the Alps to Italy. We had some bad luck as after our departure a storm started and the trip to Italy took three days and three nights instead of only one day. We squished in the deep snow and lost five people who fell into a deep chasm on the way. When we finally got to a town called Merano in Italy, we found out that the trucks that were supposed to take us to Milan had left long before we arrived. We waited one more day until new transport arrived to take us. We arrived in Milan at night and we were housed in the Jewish center at no. 5 via dell'Unione Street. We spent two days there. From there, we took a train to Rome and we were housed in the cinema city, Cinecittà.

Once in Rome, I began to trade with anything I could lay my hands on. I'd buy dollars from people coming to town and sell them to those who were leaving, I'd buy a bag of buns

---

11   The United Nations Relief and Works Agency.

and a box of salted fish in the city and at night I'd sell them to customers for double the price. With the money I earned, I traveled throughout Italy. I finished my trip in the town of Barry. Nearby, in the village of Metaponto, the 'Mossad Le Aliya Bet' organization who organized the immigrants and sent them to the land of Israel, set up a supply base for the ships leaving for Israel. Members of the 'Mossad Le Aliya Bet' gathered many hundreds of young people like me together, to prepare them to board on illegal immigrant ships. While waiting for the arrival of the ship which was to take us to the land of Israel, the people of the 'Mossad le Aliya Bet' prepared us for the event in which the British army would track us and try to board the ship. We received training on face-to-face martial arts and fighting with sticks before boarding the ships.

A few days later we were informed that the ship had arrived. Indeed, during the night of May 13, 1947 they gathered us on the beach and started to transfer us to the ship that was anchored at sea, group by group, using fishing boats. Boarding the ship was done quietly and discreetly, so that the Italian authorities wouldn't know it was happening. 1,457 people boarded that ship with me. We were taken straight down to the hull of the ship. Every one of us had been assigned a bunk only 30 cm high and 40 cm wide. We were packed like sardines in a can until everyone had been loaded and the ship began to move. For the history books, when the boat started sailing we became what are known as 'illegal immigrants' or 'Ma'apilim'.

The ship was actually a small wooden boat, which I now know was previously used for transporting cattle on the shores of Italy and Greece; It had a relatively low silhouette. The highest area was in the stern, where the ship's command area was. The deck itself included several openings for loading cattle on board, which were covered by tarpaulin. We called the ship 'Milter', a 'bowl' in Yiddish. The boat was nothing more than that, but the people of the 'Mossad Le Aliya Bet' gave her a more respectable name: The immigrants ship "Mordey Hagetaot" (the Ghettos' Fighters).

The 'Ma'apilim' ship "Mordey Hagetaot"
The picture taken from the Palyam & the Haapala site:
(http://www.palyam.org/Hahapala/Teur_haflagot/hf_Mordey_Hagetaot)

The ship set to sea secretly and without any problems. At the time, we didn't know in which direction it sailed. Later in journey we found out that it set out for the Greek Islands and from there we should have been sailing towards the south coast of Israel.

At the start of the journey the ship's crew, who came from Israel, organized us in three rings of protection, with each ring having an Israeli escort to serve as its commander. Each commander selected someone to be his deputy and he in turn teamed with a group of more than ten people.

The overcrowded conditions in the hull were very hard for all of us and we felt suffocated. As if that wasn't enough, within a few hours we started to feel sick because of the rocking of the ship and many of us began to vomit. I threw up, too. Those of us who still had an appetite could eat the daily ration we received, which included a little water, some sardines and some biscuits. Of course there were no toilets in the hull; the only facilities were one fixture on board with 'sniping services' directly into the sea. Every few hours, permission was given to go to the bathroom. The line was long and the time was always too short.

During daylight we weren't allowed to leave the hull. At night we were brought up on deck in organized groups under strict discipline to allow us to breathe a little air and throw up into the sea instead of on each other. It was forbidden to smoke and we weren't allowed to wander freely on the deck so as not to disrupt the balance of the ship because of the large weight the ship was carrying. But we were all very young and had a lot of experience in suffering from the past and the hope of arriving in Israel helped us overcome the inconveniences we faced.

Two days after the start of the journey the sea became very rough and the ship rocked from side to side at frightening angles. We were told that we should be aware that the ship could capsize. Some of the people started to call out 'Shema Israel', while others began whining. Generally, everyone felt like we were doomed.

As the storm worsened, the ship found shelter behind the island of Cephalonia for almost a day and a half. When the storm subsided, the sea became calm and I didn't suffer from seasickness until the end of the journey. Compared to the ship's rocking during the storm, the rest of the journey was very relaxed. The main problem we had to deal with after the storm, was the lack of water. I had no idea how the 'Mossad le Aliya Bet' people had calculated the amount of water loaded on the ship, but the water was running out. Despite the heat and the sultriness in the hull, each of us received only one liter of water per day.

A few more days of sailing went by (at the time I didn't know how many, because every day felt like a never-ending nightmare) and we were told that the ship came within a few miles offshore. The following day, when the ship was probably close to the town of Rafah, a British plane was seen in the sky above the ship and later that morning a British destroyer appeared. The ship's route changed to the direction of the beach of Tel Aviv. That afternoon, another British destroyer arrived and demanded that we sail to the city of Haifa. The ship's captain refused and began sailing in zigzags. It was obvious that something was happening. We realized that the British had located us. Some of the people began boarding on deck but the aisles were so crowded that I couldn't go on deck myself initially and remained in the hull along with many others who had tried and failed to get out. Just as the conflict with the British soldiers started, I managed to go out on deck. In the distance, I saw the coast of the land of Israel for the first time. People standing next to me told me that the white houses seen in the horizon were the houses of Tel Aviv. We were so close, yet still very far away.

Two destroyers had set themselves parallel with our ship between them and slowly began approaching it until they rammed both sides. The pressure created on our ship was so great that we could hear the creaking of the ship in the hull and some of the wooden beams on the deck broke. A number of people were injured at this stage. British soldiers started dangling ropes onto the deck of the ship while other British soldiers began to splash water jets and shoot tear gas at us.

When British soldiers boarded the ship, a struggle began in which we threw cans, bottles and food scraps. Many of us got badly beaten by the British, but the British got their fair share as well, even though we were very weak following our voyage at sea. A lot of blood was spilled on deck. It took the British soldiers over three hours to take over our ship. The following day they towed the ship to the Haifa harbor and we were transferred to a deportation ship called SS Ocean Vigour. We were taken down to the hull of the deportation ship and put into types of cages wrapped in nets. We moved from the hull of one ship to cages in the hull of another ship.

We had no idea where they were taking us, but when we arrived to port and they started downloading us from the deportation ship, some of us recognized the language of the people in the harbor; it was Greek. We realized we had been brought to Cyprus. After bringing us down from the deportation ship they loaded us on military trucks and accompanied by British soldiers equipped with weapons, they moved us to our new home for the next year and a half: Summer Camp No. 55 in the port city of Famagusta.

CHAPTER ELEVEN

FROM CAMP NO. 55 IN CYPRUS TO THE AIR FORCE BASE IN RAMAT DAVID, ISRAEL

Summer Camp No. 55 was a tent camp set up by the British. The camp was fenced with double barbed wire, lighting towers had been built around the camp and British sentries were sitting there on guard day and night. It was a penal camp and throughout our stay there, no more illegal immigrants arrived except for a group of several hundred 'Ma'apilim' from North Africa. The camp was closed and locked. The British prevented us from exiting the camp and made it clear that those who left without permission would be shot. I had returned to be locked in a camp again, but I couldn't compare life in this summer camp to what we had experienced in the camps during the War, even though the British soldiers treated us pretty badly.

We lived in tents. They were canvas tents that were strained using iron spikes, three pegs on each side and the opening closed with a piece of tarp. Six people lived in each tent. Each of us had a bed of his own and a cabinet for personal belongings. In the tent with me were Simcha Granot and Abraham Epstein, whom I got to know during the voyage at sea. The tent didn't have any electric lights. Summer made it very hot inside the tent and in the winter it was very cold. Some tents didn't survive the winter winds and simply tore off their spikes and flew away in the wind, and the people living in them were left exposed to the cold and the rain. When it rained, the camp became a swamp of squelching mud, which made our lives very difficult, as well as getting around camp.

At a later stage the British began to build long, tin barracks with arched tin roofs in the camp. These barracks were actually used as public buildings for residents of the camp. They were used by the management of the camp and classes were held in them including Hebrew classes, college preparations and 'Bagrut' (matriculation) classes, 'Palmach' (the striking force of the 'Hagana' organization) training, and general classes. In one of the barracks there was also a canteen. Today, the IDF (Israel Defense Forces) call it a 'Shekem'.

The food was of poor quality and even in short supply at first, until we found out that the British soldiers stole our food. Every resident received a ration of food and could choose between eating in a communal kitchen or cooking his own food on a paraffin stove, which was supplied to us. I preferred eating with a member of the group who I'd met during our voyage at sea, Mordechai Neumann. In his group, called 'Noha"m' (Consolidated Pioneer Youth), there were two girls who could make wonders with their cooking. I obviously preferred eating with them and they enjoyed my food allowance.

There was a shortage of clothes and shoes, so we had to sew our own clothing from the fabric of the tents. The water was scarce and it naturally affected our hygiene. The result of which was that we scratched chronically all over our bodies.

A management committee was set up in camp and represented the residents of the camp to the British army. My friend Mordechai Neumann, who knew Hebrew and English, was appointed to the Executive Committee in charge of bringing food from the town of Famagusta to camp. He discovered the stealing of food by the British soldiers and put an immediate stop to it.

Within a short time, representatives of the 'Palmach' reached camp and in coordination with the Management Committee of the camp, divided us into groups according to military functions. I took a course in self-defense and explosives as part of the 'Hagana' organization and became an explosives instructor. Every night we would practice and go through night training. They really had us working hard during these trainings, but they also helped us get over the boredom during the day.

Tents in Camp No. 55 (photo from the internet)

Summer Camp No. 55 in Cyprus (photo from the internet)

The fence with a double barbed wire that surrounded the camp
(photo from the internet)

Max Gutkin in Summer Camp No. 55

Max Gutkin in Summer Camp No. 55

Upon my arrival in Cyprus, I sent a letter to my cousin Rita (Schalman) and her husband Roma Paperna, whose Tel Aviv address I remembered from when I was a child for some reason: 44 Sheinkin Street, Tel Aviv. Although they had moved since, the mail was able to track them down and give them my letters. So began our correspondence through which I was able to complete some missing information.

I found out that after I'd left Germany, my father and Zhenya (Rogalin) managed to get 'certificates' under the names of the Schalman couple (Rita's parents) who hadn't survive the Holocaust, that allowed them to immigrate to Palestine legally. They arrived in Israel in early 1947 and began living in Tel Aviv.

Thus, I also heard some very sad news. After I'd left Germany, my cousin Nyoma took a ride in a tram through the streets of Munich one day. An American Military truck driver, apparently drunk, crashed into the tram, wounded many and killed Nyoma. After all the hardships he had been through, the Angel of Death got him. Olga (Rogalin), who was still in Munich, took care of his burial in the Jewish cemetery in Munich, where he is buried today.

Meanwhile, we learned of the Declaration of Independence and on the establishment of the State of Israel. The joy was great, but not for long. News of the outbreak of the Independence War frustrated us, because we wanted to participate. Even the Israeli authorities wanted that.

So, the 'Palmach' decided to smuggle me and other friends selected by the management committee of the camp, from camp. This group included my friends Simcha Granot and Mordechai Neumann. We were taught to crawl without raising any dust or making any noise, and to move along a rope hanging in the air - left leg and right arm, right leg and left arm, it's called 'the walking of a chameleon'. We were trained in this over and over, night after night. We were also told that upon our departure from camp we would have to get to the woods located about 150 meters from the camp's fence where we would have to wait for a car to pick us up. Over the months we had also been working at night, helping a crew that was excavating a tunnel under the double fence of the camp toward the woods. We would walk around camp and spread the dirt around.

It had been nearly seventeen months since we'd arrived at camp No. 55. In May 1948, after the establishment of the State of Israel, the women were released from camp and only the men remained. One evening during the Month of October 1948, 14 members from our group received an instruction to get to one of the barracks in camp; none of us knew why. When we arrived, the guide told us that we were going to escape that night. He ordered us to leave all our belongings in a tent and to just take a jacket, a shirt, pants and shoes. The guide explained to us all that it was a risky operation that could cost our lives and wanted to know if any of us did not want to go ahead with the plan. We were all silent. The excitement was immense. For the first time in a year and a half it felt like I was getting closer to my goal: to get to the land of Israel which had now turned into the State of Israel.

In the evening twilight, when the camp was still active and noisy but the sun was down, we were off on our way. One by one we went through the tunnel. Once leaving the tunnel we crawled, as trained, to the woods until we reached the trees of the woods and waited for the rest of our friends. Soon everyone had arrived. We went deeper into the woods and lay down under the trees watching the road on the other side of the woods waiting for the getaway car.

Early in the morning arrived a small Fiat car, that had all its seats taken out. We looked at each other and couldn't understand how we were all going to fit in a car so small. Eventually we managed to squeeze in, all of us together, one lying on the other, just like that. After a drive that seemed endless to me, we reached an orchard. The driver unloaded the human cargo and drove off. At the center of the orchard was a small packing house with a concrete floor. We all lay down on the concrete floor immediately. We hadn't had anything to eat for many hours, and we were thirsty and exhausted. According to the instructions we'd received before the escape, we were supposed to keep a low profile and not leave the packing house during the day. We had to tend to our needs in the orchard at night only and wait for instructions. We slept for several hours until nightfall. My stomach rumbled but I could feel a delightful sense of freedom in my heart. Fortunately, a representative of the 'Palmach' came at night with a can of water, sardines and biscuits. Since we got off the 'Mordey Hagetaot' ship, we didn't 'have the honor' of eating that standard meal. The 'Palmach' representative told us that within a few days someone would come to get us.

Thus, began our stay in the packing house at the heart of the orchard, somewhere in Cyprus. The nights were very cold and we wore poor clothes as we had been instructed and we slept close to each other. Every night we waited for someone to come and pick us up, but nothing happened. The tenth night was an especially stormy night, pouring with rain with a strong wind shaking the orchard trees intensely. Very early the following morning, a representative of the 'Palmach' arrived. He told us to clean the floor of the packing house and erase any sign of our presence there. Then he ordered us to follow him. At first light, we arrived on the shore. What we saw was a very scary sight:

A high concrete pillar was located on the beach. A rope tied to its top was connected to the top of a mast of a small fishing boat, which was rocking at sea about 30 meters from the beach. The guide explained to us quickly that each one of us had to grab the rope and use the chameleon walking method which we had practiced so much, move along the rope to the fishing boat deck and then get down to the deck and to the hull of the boat. The rope itself shook like crazy and was hard to hold on to. Even moving on the rope was scary because of the movement of the little boat's mast on one side and the turbulent waters below. When landing on deck, I found three staff members from Israel. One of them covered me with a blanket and told me to get down to the hull. With all the difficulties we eventually all managed to get on deck, soaking wet from the waves splashing at us below and the rain soaking us from above.

We waited, shivering, in the little hold, except for Mordechai Neumann who remained at the command post of the boat as the contact person, but the boat didn't move and the rocking only increased. Mordechai signaled to us that everything was fine, but nothing was fine at all. Despite its thickness, the rope we used had snapped because of the boat's rocking and before collecting the rest of the rope back to the deck, the boat's crew started the engine. The rope wrapped around the propeller of the boat, almost overturned us and made it impossible to start the engine. One of the staff members tied himself to another rope and with two friends holding the rope, went down into the cold, rough water in an attempt to free the propeller. He disappeared under water and using a knife succeeded in cutting the rope and freeing the propeller. Seeing such courage strengthened our faith in the crew's ability to bring us safely to the shores of Israel.

The ship set off on its way in a storm, literally and figuratively. It rocked up and down, swayed left and right, and at one point even drifted towards the coast of Lebanon. Mordechai Neumann refrained from telling us about this until we arrived on the shores of Israel. At some point the sea calmed. Sailing lasted a total of thirty-six hours, until we reached Bat-Galim beach in Israel at night. I finally made it to the newly born state of Israel, extremely wet but extremely happy.

At first, we were transferred to a waiting hall. Each one of us was interviewed after some waiting time and then we were left alone to wait even more. We were hungry and thirsty, but no one bothered to offer us anything to drink or eat. We had to raise our voices for someone to bring us something to eat and drink. On that same night we were all transferred to the Reception and Sorting Base in a small settlement called Pardesiya and we were drafted to the Israel Defense Forces (the IDF). I enjoyed every minute; I felt like I was fulfilling a dream.

The next morning we were separated and each one of us was taken away to a different place. I was sent to an Instructors Course in a small village called Kfar Shmariyahu and I was told, along with others, to get on the bus that was to take us there.

Shortly after the bus started driving, a car came from behind and blocked its way. A tall man wearing a military uniform got out of the car and boarded the bus. He took a sheet of paper out of his pocket and read...my name! I raised my hand and he ordered me to get off the bus.

I got off the bus and walked to the car that was blocking the bus's way. In the car, I was asked if I had any previous experience with aircrafts. "If hanging around the Aviation Aircraft Club in Riga is considered experience, then that is the experience I have", I replied. "That's great", was the answer, "Welcome to the Israeli Air Force."

The car took me to the Reception and Sorting Center of the Air Force (Kelet 9) which was in another small settlement called Tel Letwinsky. From there, I was sent to the 'Palmach' Squadron that at the time was based at a place called Yavne'el in the Lower Galilee area. At that time, the squadron had a Ranger plane that could fly about ten passengers, two Ouster British aircrafts and three American Piper aircrafts. Once arriving at the squadron, I joined a small crew of three mechanics in total. I couldn't have asked for more. I had finally arrived I in Israel, now an independent state of the Jews, and I had the privilege of working with airplanes and taking care of them, something that I'd loved doing as a child in the Riga Aviation Club.

I later found out that we were actually the first technical staff of the Israeli Air Force; I was one of the first eight aircraft mechanics in the IAF. I served in the Air Force for a total of seven years, during which time I served at the Ramat David Air Base, not knowing all the while that the land of the Gutkin Family that my father had purchased in 1929 from a delegate of the JNF, was used for the runway of the same base.

Seven years later I retired from the service in the Air Force as an aircraft mechanic and joined the national airline EL AL, where I worked for 30 years. After I retired from EL AL, I worked for a private airline called Arkia for another 14 years. What had started as an interesting amusement for me as a child had eventually become my profession. Many years later, my son Assa served on that same base as a pilot for the Israeli Air Force; the Israeli Air Force that I had a part in building. The circle had closed.

CHAPTER TWELVE

WELL DONE
Memorial Stones in the Rumbula Forest

October 2006

The indicator lights ordering passengers to fasten their seat belts came on and the plane started to glide towards landing at the airport of Riga. The view through the window of the plane was already familiar - endless plains covered with forests of trees, tall like the masts of antique sailing ships that the industry that surrounded them in Latvia helped save my father and his father during the Holocaust. I'd seen this view through the window of the plane so many times, but suddenly it was different. I felt the excitement rising and surging within me, because this time my visit was more important than its preceding ones. This time it was designed to link the past and the future together.

Zenia Falkenstein, my father's local friend, took care of the preparation of the memorial stones with the members of the Jewish community on my behalf. Zenia informed me that the stones were set in place at the memorial site in Rumbula Forest, and everyone was waiting for me to come and 'inaugurate' their placement on site. Two years had passed since my last visit to Rumbula Forest and since I'd started executing the plan to set up memorials for my father's family before I got to hear that message.

The meeting of the plane's wheels with the runway brought me back to reality. The plane had landed, taxied to the gate and stopped. The door opened, and the many passengers descend leave the plane. For the first time since I'd started visiting Riga, I felt a sense of a mission, of the weight of responsibility and exuberance.

The next day, the sky was blue and smiling without a shred of a cloud. Zenia and his dear wife Elina picked me up from the hotel in their car and we drove towards the Rumbula Forest. I immediately asked them if everything was okay and if the memorial stones were prepared, as I had requested. I knew the answer already, but I still asked. Zenia gave me his big smile and told me in a reassuring voice that everything was fine, the stones were prepared with the family names as they appeared on the list I had sent him and that he had personally checked it. When we got to the parking lot I was the first one to get out of the car and immediately started walking towards the driveway. This time the driveway seemed longer than it was in the past. It seemed endless. I was impatient to get to the memorial square. Zenia and Elina were sensitive enough to let me go ahead alone.

At first glance, there seemed to be no change in the memorial square; everything had remained as it was during my last visit there two years before. I moved slowly toward the base of the candelabra. By now I could see that the number of memory stones that the Star of David was made of, was much more. The first thought that crossed my mind was of course, 'Where are 'our' stones?' Being overexcited, I couldn't find them initially. I circled around the statue scanning the stones with my eyes, but couldn't find them. I glanced sharply toward Zenia and he gave me a gentle sign with his smiling eyes to return to the starting point, right in front of the statue. I hurried back and there, in front of the statue, right in front of me, stood three memorial stones: a memorial to the Gutkin, the Vazbucki and the Schalman families, with the engraved Latvian names of the family members who were murdered in the Holocaust. They looked just as I wanted them to look - reddish, rough, upright and italic, full of confidence but radiating sadness too.

I got down on my knees and gently stroked the letters that were engraved in each one of the stones, very slowly, one by one. I thought of my father, who knew each and every one of the family members who were now immortalized on these memory stones. He may have refused to cooperate in the setting of the stones, but he had provided the names. I was sure that despite everything, he was happy with my initiative and realized that for the first time since being murdered, they finally had a tombstone.

I stood up and stepped back to look at our three memorial stones from a distance. Now, the excitement I felt had already filled me completely. Quite unwillingly, my eyes filled up with tears at the edges, which really isn't like me at all, but I couldn't help it. I didn't notice that Zenia and Elina had approached me from behind. Zenia reached out, hugged me and said in Yiddish mixed with a little English that I had done a great 'mitzvah', and he thanked me for the honor I gave him by allowing him to help me with this. Elina wiped the tears from her eyes with her handkerchief.

The three of us stood close together, silent, each carrying his own thoughts. I thought about my grandmother Malka who I hadn't gotten to know, my uncle Reuven (Robby) who I am named after and who was murdered at the young age of 12, my uncle Ze'eva who had died from tuberculosis as a forced laborer in the Dundaga Forest and ended his life somewhere in Auschwitz and whose name, my eldest brother Ze'evi holds, and all the rest of the members of this great family who didn't have the survival capabilities and most importantly, the luck, to survive. I thought about all of these things at the same time. I also thought about my parents, my brothers, my wife and children and about myself, living as free Jews and citizens of the State of Israel and the enormous importance of the State of Israel for the entire Jewish people, just like that! I photographed the memorial stones and the entire site, and we returned to Riga.

Upon my return to Israel, I showed the pictures to my father. He looked at them for a moment and then he couldn't stop looking at them. "Well done" he said, gave the pictures back to me and said no more.

I sent the pictures to all the Schalman family members. Their excitement was great, accompanied by tears of gratitude. Once again, we felt like a big, close family, just like it had been before the War. The effort was proven right.

Seven-branched candelabrum at Rumbula forest, 2006 and memorial stones to the Gutkin, the Vazbucki and the Schalman families

CLOSING WORDS

There are many books that describe the destruction of the Jews of Latvia in World War II in detail. This book is not intended, and does not presume or attempt, to bring an historical account of these events. This is the story of Max Gutkin and of his father Samuel, from Max's personal and partial perspective according to his memoirs, many years after the events actually occurred.

To my horror, their survival story is not unique. Many people from their community experienced similar horrors and possibly even more difficult experiences. But it is the story of the Gutkin family and that makes it special for us.

The last meeting with my father regarding his survival story occurred at the end of February 2011. I asked him if there was any lesson he wished to impart to future generations. To my surprise, for the first time since he had started telling his story, my father got tears in his eyes and despite his efforts to hide it, they poked out at the edges of his eyes. He wiped his eyes and told me:

"The lesson of the Holocaust is clear and unambiguous. The state of Israel is the only refuge left for the Jews. The future generations have a sacred duty to protect it at any cost. There is no alternative and anyone who thinks that there is an alternative is misleading himself. Always remember this, and remember it well."

ACKNOWLEDGMENTS

This book could not have been published without the cooperation of my father Moshe (Max) Gutkin of blessed memory, who passed away on 16.5.2012. My father managed to read the handwritten manuscript of this book and make his comments. I was privileged to be able to thank him for agreeing to tell the full story of his rescue during the Holocaust, despite how difficult it was for him to do so, and for dedicating many Saturday mornings for this purpose. In the same breath, I would like to thank my mother Ziva Gutkin, of blessed memory, who through her wisdom gave us the opportunity that allowed my father and me to spend the time alone on the porch and engage in an effort to restore the darkest days of his life. My mother passed away on 1.6.2014.

I feel deep gratitude towards my brother, Assa. Assa accompanied me, whether in writing or the long walks through the streets of Riga, during the past eighteen years and enthusiastically joined me in my excursion of the Gutkin family's journey in Riga during the Holocaust.

I owe acknowledgments to a long list of other people who found the time to help me: Ms. Melissa Spinelli of Berghahn Publishers New York, and Messrs. Andrej Angrick and Peter Klein, authors of the book 'The Final Solution' in Riga: Exploitation and Annihilation, 1944-1941, who helped me locate the statement of my Grandfather Samuel. To my father's friend, Mordechai Neumann, who added to my knowledge about the sea voyage on the 'Mordey Hagetaot' Ma'apilim ship, about the life in Camp No. 55 in Cyprus and about the escape from the camp and the journey to Israel. To my friend Attorney Jul Bardos who translated the statement from German to Hebrew, to my friend Dan Ben-Ari who agreed to read the manuscript and make comments and helped me greatly in processing photographs that accompany this book. And of course, to Mr. Benny Carmi Who convinced me of the importance of publishing this book in English and to all the E-Book Pro team, who patiently worked on preparing the book for its publication in English.

I owe special thanks to Mr. Danny Bar-on. Without him I would not have been able to fulfill my wish of translating this book into English and enabling English readers to be exposed to the survival story of my father and my grandfather. Danny translated my book with tenacious determination and his contribution to the translation of this book is priceless. Danny is not a professional translator and his translation of this book from Hebrew to English, with my assistance, is a free translation. If any translation errors are found in this book, they are all mine alone.

Finally, I want to thank my wife, Hannah, for the patience she found while I was writing this book and later on translating it and to my children Noa, Itamar, Omer and Yuval, who allowed me to repeatedly use the computer in the basement of our home every evening, for many days.

January 2018

GUTKIN, SCHALMAN AND ROGALIN FAMILY MEMBERS WHO DID NOT SURVIVE THE HOLOCAUST:

Malka (Rabinovitch) Gutkin

Seew Gutkin (Ze'eva)

Reuven Gutkin

Boris Gutkin

Nina Gutkin

Hiena Gutkin (Gena)

Rachel Gutkin

Fanja (Rozengarten) Gutkin

Seew Gutkin (Vulja)

Benjamin Gutkin (Njoma)

Rachel (Gutkin) Vazbucki (Roza)

Zalja Vazbucki

Tina Gutkin

Lusja Gutkin

Nachum Schalman

Ljuba (Rabinovitch) Schalman

Josef (Osip) Rogalin

Max Gutkin
1925-2012

LIST OF PHOTOS

Malka Gutkin in her youth

Little Max Gutkin with his mother Malka (Mania) Gutkin

Max, Robby and Ze'eva Gutkin

Malka (Mania), Ze'eva and Samuel Gutkin

Max Gutkin giving his Bar Mitzvah sermon

The big building on the corner of Brivibas and Matisa Streets, before World War II

The big building on the corner of Brivibas and Matisa Streets, 1993

The Zunde Factory

The massacre site in Rumbula Forest, 1993

The massacre site in Rumbula Forest, 2004

Mr. Zenia Falkenstein at the entrance to the massacre site in Rumbula Forest, 2004

The Lenta plant, 2010

Samuel Gutkin, before and after WWII

The Ma'apilim ship "Mordey Hagetaot"

Tents in Camp No. 55

Summer Camp No. 55 in Cyprus

The fence with a double barbed wire that surrounded the camp

Max Gutkin in Summer Camp No. 55

Seven-branched candelabrum at Rumbula Forest, 2006 and Memorial stones for the Gutkin, the Vazbucki and the Schalman families

Max Gutkin

27609671R00111

Made in the USA
Columbia, SC
26 September 2018